INSIGH

MANAGING CONFLICT

CWR

WAVERLEY ABBEY INSIGHT SERIES

INSIGHT INTO

MANAGING CONFLICT

Chris Ledger and Claire Musters

CWR

WAVERLEY ABBEY
INSIGHT SERIES

The Waverley Abbey Insight Series has been developed in response to the great need to help people understand and face some key issues that many of us struggle with today. CWR's ministry spans teaching, training and publishing, and this series draws on all of these areas of ministry.

Sourced from material first presented over Insight Days by CWR at their base, Waverley Abbey House, presenters and authors have worked in close co-operation to bring this series together, offering clear insight, teaching and help on a broad range of subjects and issues. Bringing biblical understanding and godly insight, these books are written both for those who help others and those who face these issues themselves.

CONTENTS

Introduction

1. An introduction to conflict   10

2. Factors that characterise conflicts: inner needs and anger   34

3. Factors that characterise conflicts: our minds   65

4. Handling conflict well   76

5. Practical suggestions for conflict situations   92

Appendices   120

Notes   124

INTRODUCTION

Conflict is an inevitable and unavoidable part of life. It batters and bruises us with squabbles, with the resulting friction frequently ruining relationships. Unresolved conflict destroys families, marriages, friendships, businesses and church fellowships. These shattered relationships arise because either one or all parties involved are ineffective in conflict resolution or one party or both do not want to resolve the conflict. Conflict need not result in calamity or disaster and, when handled creatively, it can become a growth point. God's love calls us to live beyond our own limitations, and provides us with the courage to continue seeking and working for the benefit of all. He is the Father of creativity, and therefore the source of help as we seek to handle conflict well. It's a privilege to share what I have learnt about conflict, not only from my clients but also from my own experiences, and we will be looking at this subject from several angles. My desire is that this book will leave you better equipped to handle conflict creatively with God's grace and love.

Chris Ledger

This book started out as a seminar that Chris ran at Waverley Abbey House. Chris is a qualified counsellor, supervisor and trainer and her desire is to see us all learning to work and live together, being honest about our differences but dealing with conflict well and loving each other through it. My job was simply to help compile the content into book format to enable a wider audience to benefit from Chris's wisdom.

I learned a lot about my responses to conflict while putting this book together – and how I tend to allow anger to overwhelm me and cloud my overall judgement. I truly believe working on this book has given me some new and creative ways to approach conflict, and for living a godly life generally. My prayer is that it will do the same for you. No book is exhaustive, but this one is packed full of honest, helpful and wise advice that has stood the test of time. Chris has looked to biblical examples and current counselling wisdom, drawing on countless situations she has helped others with, as well as talking honestly about her own experiences.

While reading this book you will look at what conflict is, how we cope with it, what the Bible says about it, how Jesus handled conflict and what He said about it. You will also learn how to deal with the factors that characterise most conflicts (unmet needs, highly aroused emotions and distorted thoughts) as well as practical pointers on how to approach conflict resolution.

Claire Musters

CHAPTER ONE

AN INTRODUCTION TO CONFLICT

WHAT IS CONFLICT?

Stop and think for a moment. What are the words that immediately pop into your mind when you think of the word 'conflict'?

You may have thought of words such as: fighting, arguments, tensions, battle, fear, confrontation, pain, messiness, aggression, disharmony, upset and sadness. Loss could also have been in there, as could hate and control – and you will probably have come up with many difftrent words we've not listed here. For all of us it will be true to say that we've experienced conflict in a variety of ways. And some of us will feel more comfortable handling it than others. However you feel about it, conflict is an inevitable part of life.

The word 'conflict' is actually derived from two Latin words: *con*, which means together, and *fligere*, which means to strike. So the word refers to people coming together with the intention of striking one another. The term conflict is often used to describe a battle, but is also used for people throwing words, rather than weapons, at each other.

Here are two dictionary definitions of conflict. *The Collins English Dictionary & Thesaurus* says it's, 'A struggle, a battle; opposition between ideas and interests' while *Compact Oxford English Dictionary* describes it as: 'A state of opposition or hostilities; a fight or struggle; the clashing of opposed principles'.[1]

It is obvious, therefore, that conflict is a clash of something – whether it be principles, values, belief systems or simply a clash due to a lack of understanding. There are in fact, as we shall discover, many reasons for conflict.

CONFLICT IN EVERYDAY LIFE

Conflict can be both positive and negative. It is a regular part of our lives, so if we can learn to resolve it in a creative way then it can be quite positive. Indeed it can open us up to other ways of viewing things and widen our possibilities of experience. On the other hand, conflict *can* be totally destructive, spiteful and damaging to the wellbeing of those involved in it. Often it is the result of a highly self-centred and competitive attitude – one that says: 'what I feel like doing I will do'. This approach can be found throughout society, which naturally affects each of us. And every one of us also has our own ideas, opinions and needs that we bring into relationships and work situations as well. How we manage our differences with those around us will determine the quality of our relationships and lives.

So, on a daily basis, conflict may just be a nuisance but, taken to an extreme, it can do irreparable damage to families, businesses, relationships and, yes, even churches. Ruth Gledhill, religious correspondent for *The Times,* wrote quite a depressing article about the church in conflict in 2005,[2] saying that 'research suggests people leave the church because of trivial issues and conflicts rather than religious doubts'. How sad.

She continues, 'Rob Parsons, the author of Bringing Home the Prodigals, said that people stopped coming for the most trivial of reasons. He said, "It's not big doctrinal issues. Typical arguments take place over types of buildings, styles of worship, youth work. If not that, then they argue over the flower rota."'

It is important to stress here that being involved in conflict is not sinful, and having to deal with it on a daily basis does not make us bad people. We will be looking more closely at Jesus' example soon, and we will see that He definitely engaged in conflict and clashes but He was able to resolve them in very creative ways.

Conflict is a bit like anger. As we know, anger is a very normal feeling. It's part of life, and does not become sinful until we actually deal with it in a destructive way. It's the same with conflict. It is not bad in and of itself; rather it's the way we handle and resolve conflict that will determine whether or not sin creeps into the equation. It is often the unresolved conflict that causes damage. Jesus' skilful handling of power struggles demonstrates that conflict, whatever its source, is potentially creative. It is creative because it faces us with a choice: whether or not to respond in a way that is godly and promotes the kingdom of God.

ACTIVITY

Look up and work through 'Different responses to conflict' (Appendix 1). Simply go down the list and tick those actions that you recognise can sometimes be your response to a disagreement or dispute. It might help you to bring to mind an experience of conflict

– if you can't, then simply make one up to help you. It is usually best to try and keep a specific instance in mind, in order to tie in the possible feelings, thoughts and actions to something concrete.

POWER AND CLOSENESS IN RELATIONSHIPS

It is really important to understand how much power there is in relationships. In every relationship influence occurs – perhaps one person has a huge influence over the other and uses that in a particular way. Have you ever had someone bulldoze you into going one way, when you actually wanted to go another?

In healthy relationships people look at the ways in which they can help one another, but in unhealthy ones a person can try to exert power over others. Imagine if someone says to you that 'you will do what I want' or 'do as I tell you'. You then have a choice about what to do. Most of us will react in one of two ways: we might become quite negative and submissive, doing anything for a quiet life and playing the game 'peace at any price', or we might become quite negative and aggressive, asserting our rights and telling others that they can't tell us what to do. The latter will probably cause a big conflict but, in fact, both responses are really about conflict. Even when we are quiet and submissive we can be in inner conflict because we feel like we are not in control of what we really want to say or do. We are paralysed by the other's words so we can't do something creative with the conflict. In fact, if we try and avoid conflict we will find that we are simply prolonging the difficulties and making things worse.

Every relationship also has a level of closeness. Again, this can be either positive or negative. Let's consider how physical and emotional closeness can be tied together. When one person tries to be physically close to another they are saying, 'I really want to be with you'. If the other person says, 'Yes, I want to be with you too' then it can be very positive, as there is mutual enjoyment in the closeness. But there may be times when one person needs some space for themselves. The other can respond positively, saying: 'Of course you can – I'm around if you need me.' That's a healthy way of dealing with closeness – they are fine whether they are together or having space apart. However, what can happen in unhealthy relationships is that one person is quite possessive, so says something like: 'I can't stand it when you're not here, we must do this together.' There can also be co-dependent relationships, where one can't exist without the other. In such cases they will say something like, 'I don't want you to go out because I need you.' That can cause a lot of conflict. It can also be quite suffocating if one person doesn't enjoy closeness and intimacy and the other person is smothering them with attention. On the other hand, it can feel rejecting if one person needs closeness and the other person is always going off to find their own space.

So issues of power and closeness can create conflict in relationships, simply because they involve give and take between two or more people. As soon as one person is doing more giving while the other is doing more taking, it becomes an unbalanced relationship. The giving and taking is influenced by the use of negative or positive power by those involved in the relationship.

THE THREE EGO STAGES

While we are looking at the subject of power and closeness in relationships, it is worth mentioning the three ego stages. These were first described by twentieth-century psychotherapist

Dr Eric Berne, who stated that each time people converse with one another a transaction is occurring. His approach to psychotherapy, the first to dare to question Freud, was known as Transactional Analysis (TA).[3] While agreeing with Freud that every person has multiple natures, Berne refers to them as three ego stages that come into play in all of our relationships and 'transactions'. TA helps us to understand that we all think, feel and behave in three distinctly different ways, depending on the way we communicate (or transact) with people around us. These ego states are: parent, adult and child. This means that we are able to act in these three different ways and each behaviour mode is important in its own right. Which one we use depends upon the particular person we are with and it can change based on different triggers. Understanding the dynamics in a relationship can help us understand why we react in the way we do. For instance if one ego state dominates a person's relationship style to the exclusion of the other two then conflict can arise.

The parent ego state
This ego state is like having an inbuilt CD of pre-recorded, pre-judged and prejudiced rules for living. When in this ego state, we tend to copy the thoughts and behaviour of our parents. Hence the parent in us decides, without reasoning, how to react to situations, what is right or wrong, and how people should live. This ego state is filled with 'should' and 'should not' attitudes. Hence we can be judgmental, over-controlling and dominant. This is called 'the critical parent'.

We can, on the other hand, be nurturing when relating in the parent ego, but this *can* tip over into unhealthy smothering of others.

The adult ego state

This ego state acts in a rational and thoughtful way and is based more on current reality than the others. So it can be viewed as something like a human computer, drawing on factual data to make logical decisions. It's the part of us that can reason and negotiate well. It is a state involving thinking, in contrast to the feeling state of the child or the prejudiced behaviour of the parent.

The child ego state

We can all be in the child state and act like children, having fun and doing silly things. This state refers to the way our childhood feelings and impressions are felt and acted upon in daily life. We often encounter experiences that recreate childhood situations and cause the same emotions we felt in our earlier years. Hence this state can be fun and healthy, but in its most undesirable form it can completely take over a person's life. We can replay our childhood ways – becoming people pleasers, desperate for peace at any price; or become emotionally disturbed or completely rebellious.

TRANSACTIONS

Transactional Analysis has another important concept that is helpful to understand when thinking about a conflict situation – transactions. Transactions are about how people communicate and interact with one another. They are about identifying which ego state in me is talking to which ego state in you. We will all be aware that our communication with others sometimes runs smoothly like oil; it appears so easy and straightforward. But at other times, our communication can seem as if it is hitting some bumps – it is confusing, unclear and feels very uncomfortable.

It is important that we become aware of our various ego states and relate to each other on the appropriate level.

For example, if one person is relating from a parent ego state and the other from a child ego state, then this is termed a straight or complementary transaction. If, for example, a bullying, dominant boss (parent ego state) is telling his secretary that she should work through her lunch hour and she is a compliant people pleaser (child ego state), this is a straight transaction. However if the secretary relates from an adult ego state and clearly says that his request is not reasonable, then this will be a crossed transaction, with the boss becoming very angry (because he has not got his own way) and a conflict situation will arise.

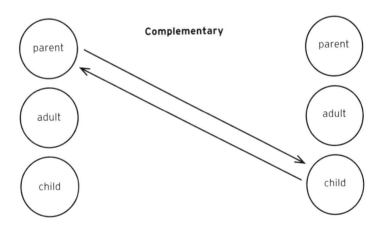

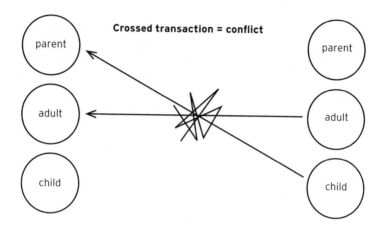

In a marriage relationship, too, there can often be one dominating figure and one submissive one. Often it is the man who is more dominating and the wife who is more compliant, but not always!

Susy was feeling very low because she felt belittled and stamped on by her husband, Richard, who somehow always managed to manipulate their differences to 'prove' he was right and she was wrong. Nothing she did was ever right, but she didn't feel she could speak to him about this. So she began to be deliberately difficult by quietly not showing any interest in him at all, even going to the extent of not cooking him his favourite food. Richard was operating from a dominating, controlling parent position, whereas she was operating from a rebellious, passive, hurt child position. Life trudged along until Susy had some counselling. Susy recognised that her quiet rebelliousness had taken root in her early years with a very vindictive and critical older sister, and that she was operating out of this rebellious, hurt child ego state. Once she was able to understand these destructive dynamics, she learnt some new communication and assertiveness skills. Slowly, over time, after many conflicts (because of the crossed transactions with Richard), as she began to initiate change he also started to modify his controlling behaviour, operating more from the adult ego and giving her more respect. This relationship could have shifted in one of two ways. It could have got much worse if Richard had refused to change – the result would have been constant crossed transactions and many conflicts. Or, as was the case, they both learned that their way of relating was unhealthy and, as they began to engage from their adult ego, their relationship improved.

JESUS: MAN OF CONFLICT

While we often think of Jesus as the one who brought peace, and obviously salvation, He in fact said that: 'I did not come to bring peace, but a sword' (Matt. 10:34) and 'Do you think I came to bring peace on earth? No, I tell you, but division' (Luke 12:51). In *The Message*, Eugene Peterson paraphrases this last verse as: 'Do you think I came to smooth things over and make everything nice? Not so. I've come to disrupt and confront!'

While Jesus did indeed call us to be peacemakers, we can learn a lot by looking at His life and seeing that, while peace may have been the intended ultimate end result, He was not afraid of addressing something that needed to be confronted and changed.

As we will see, He used conflict in a really creative way, confronting people but then helping them to move on. So let's take a closer look at some of the ways in which He created conflict:

- Even the way He was born created conflict right from the beginning. Think about the way Mary conceived and the difficulties poor Joseph had in coming to terms with it.
- When Jesus was 12 years old, He had a conflict with His parents when He stayed behind in the temple in Jerusalem after they had left (assuming He was in their party). In Luke 2 we read of His disagreement with His mother. She must have been fraught with worry: when she finally sees Him she immediately asks why He has done this to them as they have been anxiously searching. He replies: 'Why were you searching for me? ... Didn't you know I had to be in my Father's house?' (Luke 2:49). It is interesting to see how He handles this situation. He isn't being confrontational – simply speaking the truth that He has come to earth for His Father's business, and that was what He was doing.
- Jesus was tempted by Satan in the wilderness (recorded in Luke 4). But He refused to give way, combating each of Satan's attempts to use scripture to disarm Him with further scripture – thereby standing firm.
- Jesus was not afraid of conflict with the opposing religious leaders of His day. He stood up to injustice and hypocrisy and was not afraid to publicly denounce something that was wrong (see, for instance, how angry He gets in Matthew 21:12, which we will look at more closely later). Throughout the Gospels, He is locked into intermittent dialogue with the Pharisees and other religious leaders (Matthew 23 is one of the longest examples). His direct words are used to try and help them see how they are behaving – but they fall on deaf ears.
- At times He also seemed to be at odds with His disciples, although this was more about the fact that He was trying to

point out their wrong thinking and behaviour, as He similarly was with the religious leaders. His was a new way of living, and at times the disciples got it hopelessly wrong. Sometimes He seemed quite gentle in the way He responded (for example, when James and John ask to be given places either side of Jesus in heaven (Mark 10:35–45) Jesus could have exploded in anger but chose rather to teach all of the disciples about the principle of serving others). At other times He was extremely direct and clear about how He viewed a disciple's words and behaviour. For example, in Matthew 16 Jesus begins to explain what is going to happen to Him and how He must suffer. Peter, understandably not wanting this to happen, takes Him aside and says that it will never occur. But Jesus' response to Him is quite shocking to us: 'Jesus turned and said to Peter, "Get behind me, Satan! You are a stumbling-block to me; you do not have in mind the concerns of God, but merely human concerns"' (v23).

One of the keys to looking at how Jesus dealt with conflict and what we can learn from it, is the fact that He always kept His mission in mind. He came to earth to bring God's kingdom here and every conflict He caused furthered that end. That's what we always need to be aware of when dealing with conflict. If we actually want to honour God and bring about His kingdom here on earth, we need to think about how to handle conflict creatively, especially if the issue behind it is something important we feel we either need to address or stand up for.

Jesus the revolutionary

A lot of the conflict Jesus caused was because He was seen as a radical and a revolutionary. In living out His Father's purposes here on earth He overturned human lives. We can see this in Luke 4:14–30. Jesus was known in Nazareth as the 'local boy made good' but when He dared to suggest that His message would be a blessing to the Gentiles and not be reserved for the Jews alone (vv25–27), fury broke out. The people became so angry when they heard that they would not be favoured above the hated Gentiles that they tried to kill Jesus by throwing him down a cliff.

Let's be aware that as we live out our lives as Christians we may also be seen as radicals and revolutionaries. Standing against the tide of our culture will inevitably stir up conflict. Martin Luther King was a revolutionary because he fought for justice for the African-American people of America. Because he worked towards changing the status quo, people became furious with him and sadly he was killed.

As we have said, conflict is not sinful in itself – it's natural, normal and neutral, and actually, it can help us grow more into Christlikeness. From looking at Jesus' example more closely, we can see that at no point was He serving Himself. It was all about serving His Father. So to grow more like Him, the challenge is to learn how to manage conflict in a selfless way.

It is interesting to note that Jesus responded in various different ways, sometimes with real patience and at others with righteous anger. What He was doing was focusing on challenging beliefs, value systems and behaviour – not people. He wasn't trying to crush the person He was in conflict with. And that should be our approach, too. It is so important that we don't make the challenge personal but concentrate on what the other person has either said or done, rather than who they are. It isn't about attacking them, but about resolving what has happened.

ENVIRONMENTS IN WHICH CONFLICTS GROW

We can only really offer a very simplistic overview of these environments, but it is interesting to think more closely about the places where we may experience conflict.

The business world context

These days, people's energy and resources are being increasingly squeezed by having to deliver on unrealistic expectations. Often the way that bosses try to do this is through applying more pressure, bullying, accusations, or threats of redundancy. Large companies are merging with former competitors resulting in rivalry and possible redundancy – and more stress. Conflict often erupts between different workplace sectors. The result of all this? Employees become ill because of the unrealistic expectations (which means there are less people to do the jobs, therefore those that are left become even more stressed!). Direct confrontation with bosses or 'problem colleagues' is avoided because people have enough to worry about and deal with, including holding on to their job. This all places people under severe stress, which perpetuates the pressure levels at work. Additionally, workers who are stressed can, if they're not handling it well, take that stress from the workplace home to the family. This causes further conflict in the family because when someone's stressed they're on a short fuse. So stress and conflict at work actually impact on lots of other relationships outside the workplace.

Family context

In this age of economic pressure, more and more families have both parents working just to make ends meet. The downside to this is that children are generally not learning what good role models are because their parents are not around so much and also because children tend to play with the latest IT gadgets rather than interacting with those around them. This all means that the family members are reacting less together so the children aren't learning how to resolve conflict in a healthy way.

Also, the pressures and stresses of our lifestyles, as we have seen, can be brought into the home. The effect of parents' stress and arguments upon their children is well documented. For example: 'According to research, children between the ages of 6 and 17 years show signs of emotional and behavioural distress when exposed to ongoing, acrimonious exchanges and conflict between parents (see Harold, Pryor & Reynolds, 2001). Additional research indicates that exposure to this form of discord can manifest itself in a number of ways including increased anxiety, depression, aggression, hostility, anti-social behaviour and criminality (Harold, Aitken & Shelton, 2007).[4]

Social context

Just flicking the news on reveals the extent of conflict in today's world. Desperate situations in the Middle East and conflict between Protestants and Catholics in Northern Ireland are just two situations where conflict has resulted in war – and a lot of bloodshed. At the heart of each of these conflicts is a power struggle. Often it is simply both sides wanting to be in control and the abuse of power to achieve it causes huge conflict.

But it isn't just the big wars that cause conflict. A 'me-centred' view predominates in the current culture of western society. Individuals are out for their personal rights, an attitude which inevitably causes problems. We will be looking at this later, but often people are in conflict with themselves too – unhappy with the way they are. As Christians we can sometimes battle with God as well – usually because we want Him to do things in the way *we* think is best.

UNHEALTHY LEARNED BEHAVIOUR PATTERNS

Conflict can arise from both internal and external sources. How we initiate and/or cope with the conflict is usually a learned behaviour, so now we are going to look at some unhealthy behavioural patterns. These will include the following:

1. I win/you lose.
2. I want to bargain.
3. I want a quick fix.
4. I am a people pleaser.
5. I am an avoider.

We will also look at the much more healthy approach: 'I win/ you win.'

I win/you lose

This is all about scoring a victory, so those who react this way are in constant competition with the people around them. The attitude of some individuals is: 'I compete to win. I am the conqueror, I will score a victory and prove I am right and you are wrong.' They will try to out-talk those around them; they are critical, sarcastic, blame everyone else but themselves, use emotional threats (ie if you don't do this I will end our relationship), and they also use 'you' statements. The latter is very confrontational, and includes statements like: 'You always do this' and 'You're just like your mother.' Conflict for such people becomes a battle to be won, something necessary to attain dominance in a relationship and something to weaken the other person, because they always need to be in control and be the top dog.

This behaviour is very evident in some divorce settlements, in which one party does everything possible to give the impression that the partner is at fault; it can also become a way of punishing the partner.

It can be evident, too, in the workplace where power is attached to position, so the boss becomes bullying and belligerent. 'However long this piece of work has taken you, you will do it again and have it on my desk first thing in the morning' is typical of this behaviour – even when this is totally unrealistic and means staying up until midnight to get it done. In such an instance the boss is effectively saying, 'I win, you will do as I say.' Such people enjoy causing friction and exerting power over others.

I want to bargain

Haggling over goods in an African market stall can be fun when we're on holiday, but when we use a bargaining approach with others (ie when demands and interests are traded in), it is not an effective way to resolve conflict. Conflict resolution is not defined by how much each party concedes.

Imagine a scenario in a home in which the husband gets cold and likes the thermostat to be set at 22°C, whereas his wife gets really hot and is comfortable at around 18°C. They spend endless days fighting over the thermostat until they finally agree that one day the thermostat will be set so that it is comfortable for her, and another day so that it is comfortable for him. You can imagine how uncomfortable they both are with this. Each conceded the same amount, and to the bargainer that is what conflict resolution is all about, so neither feels they won. While bargaining can sometimes be the only way forward it isn't the best – it would have been far better if they had compromised on setting the thermostat at 20°C.

I want a quick fix

We live in an instant society in which technological advances, such as the internet, mobile phones, etc, have enabled us to get pretty much what we want when we want it. Similarly, when faced with conflict, some of us naturally reach for whatever quick fix solution we can find.

Putting a sticky plaster on an infected wound is not healthy, as it needs to be cleaned up and aired. In the same way this sticky plaster approach is not effective for conflict. Very often what underlies the desire for a quick fix is fear: fear of losing control (with the underlying threat that felt emotions may become overwhelming), fear of showing oneself vulnerable (with the horror that others may perceive you as weak) and/or fear of being perceived as a failure.

So people look for a quick fix in conflict situations because they don't want to face their fear. In reality they are choosing to go along with something that they don't really want to, and they are fuming on the inside. However, they choose that route rather than being honest because they believe it will protect them from an inner fear that they can't really handle. Sometimes we actually choose quick fixes to protect ourselves, but tiptoeing around issues and putting a sticking plaster on an increasingly nasty wound is detrimental for all concerned.

I am a people pleaser

Being a people pleaser is another type of quick fix. Such people give in, act like martyrs, go silent, hide their feelings, pretend and become resentful. Chris explains: 'My way of coping in my early years was to be a people pleaser. I grew up in a family where my sister was very controlling. She was my twin sister, half an hour older than me – and she let me know it as well. My mother was also very dominating and controlling so I learnt to play the game. I learnt to survive by maintaining the peace at any price. I was the easy one in the family and people used to say "Chris will do it." But actually that doesn't help resolve conflict. I've learnt over the years to resolve conflict with my husband in a much healthier way. He now says that since I've done counselling training I've changed for the better!'

The cost of being a people pleaser is that our emotions, particularly anger, can be suppressed and resentment can grow like a cancer. Hence this is not a healthy way to interact.

I am an avoider
It is tempting, if we bury our head in the sand, to believe that conflicts will just go away and we can pretend they don't exist. We sometimes retreat and escape from the conflict intentionally. Often people use this approach because they don't have the confidence to deal with the conflict or they don't have the energy. Perhaps they mistakenly think that time will heal all wounds or that by ignoring the problem it will disappear. But, as we've already said, it actually makes things a whole lot worse.

Others recognise that there is conflict, yet refuse to confront the other party because confrontation can be perceived as ungodly and unfriendly, because it is a battle in which they feel someone will come out as a loser or they fear that they may be rejected as a result. Interestingly, churches can be places where confrontation is not handled well, and yet, as we have already seen, Jesus did not shy away from conflict. By keeping hold of the irrational belief that conflict is always negative we can miss out on growing as a person.

We often think it is easier to ignore differences and swallow our anger instead of addressing issues. Often we worry that trying to discuss controversies openly may end up destroying any goodwill that remains. We fear disagreement. This, of course, does not have to be the case.

WHY DO PEOPLE AVOID CONFLICT?

We've already touched on this but it is basically because of underlying fear – the fear of coming across as unfeeling, cold and inhuman, or of being seen to behave aggressively. Alternatively, we may fear we could be rebuffed, hurt, rejected and destroyed. Therefore we suppress feelings and retreat into isolation.

Again, as we've seen, some of us falsely believe that conflict always brings destruction. We may also feel that it drains our energy, so we decide it is far better to keep away from it!

WHY ARE PEOPLE AGGRESSIVE?

Often those who come across as really aggressive (the 'I win/ you lose' people) don't always feel that good about themselves – they have low self-esteem. The term 'self-esteem' refers to the way we view ourselves; the thoughts we have about ourselves and the value we place on ourselves as people. Hence when we don't feel good about ourselves and have little self-belief, we lack confidence. People lacking in confidence can be considered by others as insecure and weak, so this obviously does nothing for their self-esteem. Consequently, people try to compensate for their low sense of self by controlling and dominating others.

This gives more of a feel good factor and momentarily raises their self-esteem – with destructive consequences.

Such people choose to act offensively, preferring to suffer or inflict pain rather than leave the scene. To them, conflict increases their sense of vitality – they like the adrenalin buzz that the emotional arousal of conflict brings. Some people actually become addicted to being angry most of the time, because it gives them such an adrenalin buzz. Indeed, while attending a day's conference on anger management, Chris noted that the tutor, a clinical psychologist, said that anger can become addictive as it gives people the same buzz as having an orgasm. They become macho because they like the feeling.

THE HEALTHY WAY TO PERCEIVE CONFLICT: I WIN/YOU WIN

Of course, in any conflict resolution the healthy way is to work together to find a way forward. This approach says, 'I value you and affirm you, and I want to hear what's going on for you. Let's see if we can come to some compromise by sharing our thoughts and feelings about this situation with one another.' Within this approach people will negotiate, clarify, try to understand, maybe agree to differ, use 'I' statements, share feelings, compromise and come up with a resolution with which everyone is happy.

This healthy way of perceiving conflict says:
- There is energy around; I will channel it in a positive way.
- Conflict helps me to break out of unhealthy patterns.
- Working out differences benefits everyone.
- Conflict can be a growth point.

ACTIVITY

How do you usually regard conflict? Are you a winner/loser, bargainer, quick fixer, people pleaser or avoider? Now think about a particular conflict that went badly wrong and how you tried to resolve it. Why didn't your approach work?

WE ARE WHOLE PEOPLE

It is important to become self-aware, because until we understand how we act in conflict and what our coping mechanisms are, we can't really make any changes within ourselves and thus resolve things well. Every human being is designed by God to function in five specific areas and this book gives us a biblical understanding based on the Waverley model (see Appendix 2). We are all physical beings, we all have emotions, we make choices about how we behave, we have the ability to think things through and we are spiritual beings. Therefore, addressing conflict will affect every part of our beings, including the spiritual. Here is a brief summary of the five areas:

- Spiritual: we see this as our inner core, where deepest longings and thirsts are located.
- Rational: everything involved in our thinking selves, such as specific thoughts, beliefs, values and plans.
- Volitional: makes the connection between what we are thinking and the end goals we hope to achieve. It is here that we make choices about how to behave.
- Emotional: the area that covers our feelings. Often these can signal where our difficulties lie (and are therefore very helpful for counsellors).
- Physical: we are all physical beings and the healthiness of our bodies is not due just to illness or disease, but also to the effect

of all other areas of our functioning as humans. Sometimes our emotional state or belief pattern can affect us physically just as physical dysfunction such as illness, lack of sleep or unhealthy diet can impact our sense of spiritual wellbeing.

1 Thessalonians 5:23 says, 'May your whole spirit, soul and body be kept blameless at the coming of our Lord Jesus Christ.' This is a great, broad picture of how each of us is made – spirit, soul and body. Selwyn Hughes, who founded CWR with his theory of personality upon which the Waverley model is based, said that the 'soul' refers to our thoughts, feelings and decisions – in other words, mind, emotions and will. This three-dimensional model of the nature of humans will help us to understand conflict in a deeper way. If one part of us is not healthy then it will affect everything else. So, if we are diseased spiritually, then all other areas of our lives will be affected.

Think about an apple for a moment. Sometimes you cut it open only to find that it's going bad in the middle. Inevitably, if you had left that apple for a bit longer, it would have started going bad all the way through. This is a good demonstration of what can happen to the different aspects of our lives. For instance, if you're not handling your emotions well then it can affect the way you are thinking and feeling – which can then have a knock-on effect on your behaviour. As we are spiritual, whole beings, all five areas of functioning are usually affected when we are involved in any sort of conflict. The first sign that we are facing a conflict situation is when we start sensing a change in our body, ie tension in our stomach or hot clammy hands, and then our emotions become aroused with uncomfortable feelings. Our thoughts will also begin to change; they may become distorted and we may start feeling the need either to get confrontational or to run away and hide. Try the activity below to see how conflict can affect your whole self.

ACTIVITY
Think of a time when you faced a conflict situation, and what areas of human functioning were affected during it. Look at Appendix 2 to help you with this and also try to think about exactly how you felt in that situation. Put yourself back there and think: What emotions am I experiencing? What thoughts are going through my mind? How am I choosing to behave? Am I feeling physically sick? Is my heart racing? Am I feeling stressed and tense? And how am I affected spiritually? Is my sense of self, security, and value being wobbled?

REFLECTION
Now that we have looked at what conflict is, where it can occur and unhelpful learned behavioural responses to it, reflect on how conflict makes you feel generally. Do you cope with it well or tend to avoid it? Have you had positive experiences or is your experience usually negative? How did you feel when learning that conflict is neutral and that Jesus engaged in it? At this point do you truly believe that conflict can help you grow as a person?

PRAYER
Lord, help me to understand that each one of us is made in Your image. You have created us to be whole. Help me to be open and honest about myself, and the areas that need work, as I continue to read through this book.

CHAPTER TWO

FACTORS THAT CHARACTERISE CONFLICTS: INNER NEEDS AND ANGER

UNMET INNER NEEDS

- As spiritual beings we all have a thirst. To understand this further, let's talk in terms of a physical thirst. If I thirst for water I can't describe the feeling precisely, apart from having a dry mouth. However, I know I can't simply just press a button to have my thirst quenched; I've got to do something about it. I've got to choose to go to the cupboard to get a glass for the water and then take it to a tap to fill it with water before drinking it to quench my thirst. If I was in a desert somewhere without a water source I would become desperate because water is a basic human need.

At a much deeper level we each have basic spiritual thirsts and needs. God created us in communities, and meeting one another's needs, to some extent, is critical to the wellbeing and development of any relationship. God supplied us with the need to feel that we belong somewhere.

When children are brought into families it's really important that families embrace them and they feel that they belong in those families in order to gain a sense of security. It's also important that they feel a sense of self-worth. We all need affirmation, especially as children. Children need to be told that those around them are very proud of them and that they will be loved whatever they do.

We also have a need to feel significant and to feel we've a part to play in our families, workplaces etc. Each of these deep spiritual thirsts, the need to feel security, self-worth and significance, are reasons why God put us in families in our early years. Our emotional tanks are empty when we are born but they get filled up in a loving, fully functioning family. Research in places like Romania shows us how important this actually is. In Romanian orphanages it has been found that when children feel abandoned rather than loved and cared for they don't develop security and a sense of worth and, as a result, don't survive very well.[5]

Of course many of us do not experience perfect parenting, as no one is perfect, but some will have had their emotional and spiritual tanks filled up more than others. Whatever your experience has been, you will still be thirsting for something – to a particular degree – as we're always thirsty. We learn that often we need to do something in order to quench that thirst. Just as we couldn't simply press a button to rid ourselves of that deep thirst for water, if we want to feel good about ourselves we can't just press a button and feel a sense of worth. We have to behave in a certain way to move towards the goal.

Blocked goals

- Imagine Jane as a people pleaser. She felt her parents loved her, and she gained a sense of self-worth through being an easy, rather than difficult, member of the family. However, when Jane came across a difficult situation at work the same approach didn't work. She couldn't actually please her boss because he was quite difficult and bullying. However hard she tried to please him, it didn't cut any ice and she came up against a 'blocked goal'. This simply meant she couldn't reach her goal (to please him), which would then have filled her emotional and spiritual tank up. The result? Jane began to feel really upset, angry and very insecure deep inside about who she was. Consequently her choice was to behave in a way that avoided the situation, and her thoughts turned to phrases like 'well, I'm no good anyway, I can't please anyone'. This began to affect her self-esteem, making her feel worthless, and tipping her into a low mood and depression. Burying these feelings inside, Jane started to seethe and resent her boss, even though she would actually like to have confronted him and talked the conflict out. However, she didn't because her default button was to avoid conflict in order to feel safe. She chose to meet her deep spiritual need for self-worth in the wrong way.

Let's think of another example. Supposing Rachel's goal is to control everyone. She works in a team and feels the need to tell each individual exactly what they should do. Rachel uses very driven words, such as 'should', 'must' and 'ought', trying to project a sense of being in control. What she is actually doing is looking for a sense of significance, because when the tasks she has set have been finished, she will feel important. But if people won't do what she's said, and her goal gets blocked, she will end up feeling really frustrated and angry. A full-blown conflict will doubtless ensue.

More often than not, such conflicts arise out of the fact that we are looking to another person to meet our *spiritual* needs rather than looking to God. We need to learn to bring God into the equation in our everyday situations. Jane, for example, could have said to herself: 'Well, even if I can't please my boss, I know that in God I am a person of self-worth because Jesus has died for me on the cross and I'm really important to God. That's what matters, because my whole life is about pleasing God, not about other people.' And Rachel could have said to herself: 'Actually, God is in control and maybe it's important that my colleagues take responsibility and get on with the jobs that need doing. I can't control and dominate them to make them do what I want because it is God who is in ultimate control.'

Because basic needs are not being met in God, some people may compensate by continually judging and criticising others to try and shape them into the people they want them to be.

Roger had been married for fifteen turbulent years to Anne. Their conflicts were characteristically centred around the fact that Roger wanted to decide the way his wife had to live – he only felt secure when she was doing things his way. He hadn't learned to find his security in God. He wanted to mould Anne into the sort of wife he thought she should be. When she did anything outside his way of working he went ballistic! In spite of being constantly criticised, Anne fought hard to hang on to her own identity by standing firm in the conflict situations.

She tried to negotiate a way forward with no success because Roger didn't think there was anything wrong with the way he was behaving. In his eyes, it was all his wife's fault. Fortunately Anne had a strong faith and continually tried to draw on God's unconditional love, which helped her to feel strong enough to survive the difficulties. Sadly Roger never learned to handle conflict constructively. How did their marriage work out? It remained very uncomfortable but at least Anne felt much better about herself. Her self-esteem grew as she worked at meeting her spiritual needs in God. She also grew in confidence with the skills she had gained, and learnt not to take on board all the criticism her husband threw at her.

As we have seen, when we perceive that having a need met by another human being is essential to survival and development, conflicts over needs can be quite serious. The truth is that God is longing for us to look for our sense of self-worth, significance and security in Him. Indeed, this is what He is talking about in Jeremiah: 'My people have committed two sins: They have forsaken me, the spring of living water, and have dug their own cisterns, broken cisterns that cannot hold water' (Jer. 2:13). They were looking elsewhere, rather than to the source that would quench their spiritual thirst. When we look to achieving goals in ways such as those outlined above, it's like we're digging cisterns that will not hold water. They won't stand the test of time because we're looking in the wrong direction for fulfilment of our spiritual needs.

ACTIVITY

Identify the blocked goal in the conflict situation you have been bringing to mind. What deep spiritual need was not being met?

Different types of needs

- It is important to recognise the needs of ourselves and others. As we've already seen, God has given us needs (such as the need for intimacy, friendship, connection etc) and there's nothing wrong with that. Often we think that people are simply either completely selfish or completely selfless, rather than a mix of both. Indeed, in an effort to appear selfless, some Christians can mistakenly hold the opinion that it would appear selfish to have needs, so they deny them. This selfless syndrome creates serious conflict.

God doesn't expect us to live as totally selfless people. If being nice and putting others' needs before our own equates to our highest aspirations to be a good, kind Christian then this becomes self-enhancing. However, we may be very successful in making others happy, but feel miserable inside. If we cannot voice our own needs we are not being real and authentic Christians and the price we pay is huge – usually a deep burning resentment burns away that, at some point, erupts into conflict. A denial of one's own needs with conflict avoidance is not an ingredient of a healthy relationship.[6] What we must try to do is have a rounded view of needs, knowing that they're only met to a certain extent in other relationships. We can't have our needs *fully* met in any other relationship than in God.

People can desire something so strongly that they interpret the desire as a need. As we struggle to make sure these 'needs' are met, conflict erupts. When the needs of both parties appear incompatible, serious conflict can arise. Further, when we ignore the needs of others, our own needs or the needs of a relationship, discord arises.

SELF-INTEREST

- Self interest, egocentricity, narcissism, egoism, call it what you will, is the root of the most destructive types of conflict, as individuals are totally centred on themselves and therefore give little ground to those around them. 'Self' words include self-centred, self-willed, self-determined, self-serving, self-absorbed and self-worshipping – and there are many more. The truth is that we can all be fiercely independent and want to be in the driving seat of our lives. Just taking a look at some biblical examples shows us that this is the case. In Luke 22:24 we find Jesus' disciples 'bickering over who of them would end up the greatest' (*The Message*) and two of the first missionaries, Paul and Barnabas 'had such a sharp disagreement that they parted company' (Acts 15:39).

Indeed James challenges us:

'Where do you think all these appalling wars and quarrels come from? Do you think they just happen? Think again. They come about because you want your own way, and fight for it deep inside yourselves. You lust for what you don't have and are willing to kill to get it. You want what isn't yours and will risk violence to get your hands on it.

'You wouldn't think of just asking God for it, would you? And why not? Because you know you'd be asking for what you have no right to. You're spoiled children, each wanting your own way' (James 4:1–3, *The Message*).

When thinking about conflict it's vital we recognise the issue of our fallen nature and note that Satan is out to disrupt and destroy. He will get between relationships where and when he can, but we also often want our own way. It's important to acknowledge this human tendency and take responsibility when and where appropriate. This type of egocentricity is exactly what caused Adam and Eve to disobey God in the Garden of Eden. Satan played on the fact that God had told them they couldn't eat from the tree in the middle of the garden, focusing on the one negative because he knew that human nature would be curious and want to know why they had been denied something. Looking in Genesis we can see he says to Eve, 'God knows that when you eat from it your eyes will be opened, and you will be like God, knowing good and evil' (Gen. 3:5). Eve, eager to have that knowledge, eats the fruit and persuades Adam to do the same. Their selfishness is revealed even further when God finds them and they seek to blame everyone else but themselves for what has happened. The result? They are banished from the Garden, from enjoying God's presence freely. And that's the result of unresolved conflict too – distance creeps in between God and us.

Most of us do a good job in covering up our human bias towards independence and self-centredness. But let's just dwell on it a little longer by thinking about how siblings can squabble. A lot of the arguments children have are because they perceive a situation is unfair – and we, as adults, can still have this tendency (as indeed Adam and Eve did when they were told not to eat the fruit). Often we hear children saying the angry words, 'It's not fair' and see them hitting out at a sibling. And we can still find ourselves thinking life is unfair as adults. This can cause us to hit out at those around us – and at God too.

Deep inside each one of us there is a corruption that eats away, polluting our thoughts, words, action and our will – and affecting our choices. The result is that we tend to look in the wrong direction for our deep spiritual needs to be met, rather than looking to God and having them met in Him.

What God actually wants is for us to grow more and more dependent upon Him and less upon ourselves – that's the aim of discipleship. But of course we are 'I' dependent. Sometimes we need to stop ourselves and ask where God is in the midst of a conflict, and, rather than pushing our own opinions and desires, ask God what He wants out of it. Indeed, sometimes God allows us to be in situations of conflict because He wants to change us to be more like Christ. Perhaps we need to work on a particular aspect of our personality – we've all heard the amusing anecdote of someone praying for more patience and so God puts the person in situations that try their patience to the limit so that they can develop it!

Self-centred attitudes give rise to:
- Idealistic demands
- Unrealistic expectations
- Egotistical and arrogant attitudes
- Lack of acceptance of others' personalities
- Strong preferences (or inflexible preferences).

These human qualities can occur in churches, just as much as in other organisations. For example, pride can cause us to make arrogant assumptions (such as 'everyone should think and agree with me'). Arrogance and pride can say 'if you don't agree with me, you are flawed and wrong'. Any healthy community/team will include people who love precision and order as well as spontaneous types who like to 'go with the flow'.

There are all sorts of people in this world, and churches should be a reflection of that. In fact, everywhere you go you will come across people with different personality types. It's essential that we learn to accept one another rather than feeling threatened by someone who seems to have a different personality to us. We need to show one another grace at all times – if someone isn't gracious in return then that is their responsibility, not yours.

It's important to be aware of the impact that our own personality type has on other people. Let's look at some examples of how differing personality types can cause us to make wrong assumptions about one another. Starting with a biblical example, a lot of the tension found between Mary and Martha was due to the fact that they had very different personalities (Luke 10:38–42). Martha was a doer while Mary was content to simply sit at Jesus' feet and listen to him. Does this type of tension resonate for you?

No doubt in your church there will be all sorts of different people: the thinkers and feelers, the extroverts and introverts as well as sensing people and intuitives.

It can be just as easy for the 'feeler' to boil inside like a pressure cooker and to assume that 'thinkers' are too black and white as it is for the 'thinker' to dismiss the 'feelers', assuming that they are over-indulging their emotions. It's also easy for introverts to dismiss extroverts, complaining that 'they are so loud, and thoughtless; so demanding and draining to be with'. On the other hand, extroverts can accuse introverts of not engaging in group discussions or of being stand-offish and hard to get to know. It can also be easy for sensing people to perceive intuitives as too dreamy, 'so heavenly minded that they are no earthly good' or conversely for intuitives to accuse sensing people of being pernickety with facts.

Can you see how easy it is for our self-centredness to cause us to become unaccepting of others – even fellow Christians? And yet the Bible reminds us that God has called, indeed needs, all of us: 'all of you together are the one body of Christ, and each one of you is a separate and necessary part of it' (1 Cor. 12:27, TLB).

Healthy relationships are built upon acceptance of differing personality types. Unhealthy relationships that struggle with conflict probably have difficulty in accepting that we are all different at their root. But wouldn't it be boring if we were all the same? Most conflict arises because specific differences between individuals are not recognised and acknowledged. When Chris is involved in couple counselling one area of her work is to help the couple identify their differences and to explore whether they are accepting each other in these areas. Such differences mainly occur in five areas:

A difference in interests This is the difference between what two people actually enjoy and want. For example, one managing director may want to branch out in one way, and another in a totally different way because of their personal interests.

Ted was an entrepreneur who had built his Christian accountancy firm up from nothing. He had a keen interest to alleviate Third World poverty and decided to give money from the firm to this cause. Terry's interest, however, lay elsewhere. He wanted the firm to give away money to his cause, which was supporting an orphanage in Romania. Although Terry was only an employee, he didn't want to go along with what interested his boss and so a conflict ensued, which started to pollute the whole atmosphere of what had been a very happy firm.

A difference in understanding This is often inevitable because two people who, say, work together, have usually been brought up in different environments, in different ways, in different places and they have different life experiences, so they are bound to see things from a slightly different angle. It can happen with married couples, and also between friends.

One woman described to Claire how, as an Asian woman brought up in England, she can sometimes understand the way things are done differently to how some of her Asian friends understand them. She says: 'I often find that other Asians, mostly those who have not been brought up here like I was, expect me to be just as laid back as they are with regards to hospitality and punctuality and they simply have very different boundaries to me. So I had an instance where some Asian friends turned up two hours late for lunch, brought someone I had never seen before, and stayed for hours. They obviously thought this was acceptable and moreover that I would be fine with it as I am Asian like them. But my boundaries were different to theirs; I felt totally taken advantage of.'

A difference in expectation This can cause a high degree of conflict if not discussed.

> Before Chris got married, her husband assumed that she would work full time as a nurse but she thought otherwise, wanting part time work. Their expectations were poles apart. Having a frank and honest discussion and coming to a mutual agreement avoided a conflict later on in their married life. Chris ended up going back to nursing part time and after a year or so her husband acknowledged that this had been a very good decision. A conflict was constructively avoided by addressing their different expectations of each other's roles early on in their relationship.

A difference in value The value between what is important to one party and what is important to the other is also a big area of potential conflict.

> A wife decides to go topless on a beach and doesn't understand why her husband doesn't like it because it isn't physically hurting him – her value system says there is no problem with it. However, he could say, 'My value system's very different. It upsets me because I feel your body is for you and me to share – I'm not going to put up with you displaying it to everyone.' The wife would need to decide whether she is going to honour her husband's value system, and the husband would need to decide whether he is going to change his stance or not. If both refuse to budge, then conflict will arise.

A difference in style This simply means the different ways that we do things. There is no right or wrong, just different styles, but conflict occurs when another won't accept, or validate, the other person's style.

Claire has found this particular area highlighted since she and her husband have had children. Each of them has come across situations in which their partner is parenting in a way that is totally different to the approach they would use. Obviously their values and what they want to teach their children have already been discussed and prayed about, but sometimes the way they go about modelling those things can be very different - and Claire can sometimes be caught on the hop, finding she gets hot under the collar because her husband is doing something differently to the way she would. Actually though, it's just a difference in style. They are basically on the same page but they approach some things differently. Claire has had to learn to give her husband the space to do that, as it means their children have a more rounded upbringing. She has had to recognise that her way isn't the only way to do something.

A difference in opinion This is the difference between what two people think. A mature relationship allows both spouses to beg to differ or one person has the grace to lay aside their opinion in order to help the other.

A friend of Claire's shared how she realised she and her husband had very different opinions on a miscarriage she suffered. She saw it as a lost pregnancy and a lost baby (it was incredibly early on) but her husband saw it as a pregnancy that never happened – there was no baby even formed to be lost. The woman was totally gutted to discover that her husband felt that way and this caused a rumbling conflict between the pair of them. However, when she received counselling, they were encouraged as a couple to name the baby, put together a box of anything they had bought and commit it all back to God. Her husband was happy to do this, setting his opinion aside to help his wife to heal and move on.

ACTIVITY

- Out of the six areas of difference (interests, understanding, expectations, values, styles and opinions), which do you think fed into the specific conflict situation that you have been bringing to mind?

INTENSE EMOTIONS, PARTICULARLY ANGER

- Often conflicts get out of hand due to a rise in intense emotions. These can become real battles when we allow our feelings and emotions to become the motivators of what we say and do. This can be really unhealthy and often an explosion of anger occurs because of a whole host of frustrated feelings below the surface. An alternative is to bury our feelings through fear that they will become out of control; another unhealthy approach. We can also try to intellectualise them, which means we are not being honest about our conflict. So it is really important that we identify the emotions involved in conflict, and learn to ensure they do not drive it.

What is anger?

Anger is an emotional response to pain; a symptom of fear and hurt. It functions in the following ways:

- Anger helps us locate our wounds.
- Anger helps us to defend ourselves.
- Anger helps us to identify our blocked goal and recognise what inner spiritual need is not being met in our relationship with God.
- Anger can energise us to correct what needs correcting.

The Bible does warn us to be careful about our anger: '"In your anger do not sin": do not let the sun go down while you are still angry, and do not give the devil a foothold' (Eph. 4:26). Notice Paul is not telling us that it is wrong to be angry; rather he advises us to try and sort out our conflicts each day so that we do not take the emotion to bed with us, allowing it to fester and cause problems.

Of course, anger can trigger all sorts of uncontrolled emotions that are as terrifying as an electrical storm. Joyce Huggett, in her book on conflict,[7] says: 'Thunder claps rumble round our mind; its lightning terrifies our soul, its gale-force wind howls through our senses, its hail-stones lash our bodies, leaving us helpless. Yet just as an electric thunderstorm is often precisely what is needed to clear the air of humidity and oppressive heat, so anger is often necessary to clear our minds, cleanse our hearts and calm our fears.'

That is a great description of anger. While it can seem overwhelming and scary, if we use anger constructively it can be a cleansing agent. As Joyce Huggett says, 'It *can* ripen into a sweet fruit, or become a sour one. Everything depends upon what we do with it.' In conflict we should be asking God how we can work with Him to bring about good fruit in the place we are – whether at home or the workplace.

A biblical understanding of anger

* God's anger is mentioned 455 times in the Old Testament and 375 in the New Testament, so He definitely gets angry! And, as we considered earlier, Jesus was not afraid of conflict and He certainly got angry. The obvious example is when He arrived at the temple and found money exchangers alongside men selling animals for sacrifice. Just look at His reaction to that scene:

> On reaching Jerusalem, Jesus entered the temple courts and began driving out those who were buying and selling there. He overturned the tables of the money-changers and the benches of those selling doves, and would not allow anyone to carry merchandise through the temple courts. And as he taught them, he said, 'Is it not written: "My house will be called a house of prayer for all nations"? But you have made it "a den of robbers"' (Mark 11:15–17).

Jesus was demonstrating what we call 'righteous' anger – people were using His Father's house for their own sinful means and He was determined to do something about it. There will be times when it is right for us to stand firm in the midst of ungodly behaviour, but how we do it is really important – go back to the passage in James that we looked at in *The Message*: 'You lust for what you don't have and are willing to kill to get it. You wont what isn't yours and will risk violence to get your hands on it' (James 4:2). Earlier in his book James also says: 'human anger does not produce the righteousness that God desires' (James 1:20).

This is negative, destructive anger, which can be caused either by allowing your emotions to get on top of you, or by allowing it to seethe in cold anger as you try to suppress your emotions. Again, Jesus shows us that it is possible to own our feelings without being controlled by them. While He did overthrow tables (presumably in an act of disgust), He then went on to teach them in a calm and controlled manner.

Jesus acknowledged His feelings – and took them to God

- Let's look at a scene, just before Jesus is arrested and recounted towards the end of Matthew, in which He really did show His deepest emotions. Taking His three closest and most trusted friends into the Garden of Gethsemane, He begs them to stay with Him; to watch and to pray because 'This sorrow is crushing my life out' (Matt. 26:38, *The Message*).

Jesus takes His inner conflict to His Father. Having named and owned His inner pain, He agonises but then, with huge integrity, reiterates the deep desire that has governed His whole life: 'Yet not as I will, but as you will' (v39).

So what can we learn from Jesus? To take our inner conflicts to God. Let's make it a habit to spread out our tangled emotions before God, then dwell in His presence until an awareness of His understanding seeps in. We can then receive His love as a balm to the hurt, allowing it to calm the panic and soothe the rejection. Be assured that God is always there for us: 'Cast all your anxiety on him because he cares for you' (1 Pet. 5:7). Then, from this place, we are in a far better frame of mind to try and sort out the conflict that we were having.

ACTIVITY

- When were you last angry in a conflict situation?
- Did you want others to suffer for it?
- Did you want to intimidate them and force them into submission?
- How do you think you would have reacted in that situation had you taken the time to go to God with your frustration and hurt first, before speaking to the person involved?

Unrighteous anger

- We have seen that Jesus displayed righteous anger, but, obviously, anger can also be hugely destructive. Here we are going to look at the characteristics and causes of unrighteous anger.

Unrighteous anger is basically self-centred in its approach. Selwyn Hughes once said that: 'If you could take self-centredness out of the human heart, you would in a stroke remove the main cause of anger and thus the main cause of unhealthy conflict.' Wow, that's a powerful – and insightful – statement, isn't it?

When hurt, people often react with a desire to retaliate and hurt others back, causing conflict. Let's take a look at a psalm, believed to have been written by David when the Philistines seized him in Gath.

In Psalm 56 it says, 'All day long they twist my words; all their schemes are for my ruin. They conspire, they lurk, they watch my steps, hoping to take my life' (vv5–6). David goes on to say, 'do not let them escape' (v7). *The Message* reads: 'Pay them back in evil! Get angry, God! Down with these people!' So what do you think was going on in David's mind at this point? And what do you think his goal was?

Yes, David wanted God to destroy his enemies. He was caught, angry, in a mess, and he wanted revenge. He was also concerned that God might not do exactly what he wanted (which would result in a blocked goal). He seems slightly insecure and panicky here – his response? To demand something of God: 'do not let them escape'. He's assuming that God won't be happy about the incident, but he doesn't know for sure that God will destroy the bad guys, does he? That's what he wants, but we all have to leave what actually happens up to God. And that's what unrighteous anger finds so difficult to do.

Unrighteous anger exhibits three characteristics:

- Demandingness: I want what I want and I want it now.
- Vindictiveness: a determination to hit back at someone or something that has interfered with a certain desire, need or goal.
- The urge to control or suppress other people's choice: a desire to coerce and bully, becoming an arrogant abuser, thus limiting the freedom of others.

We've already noted that David was demanding something from God, but he was also a bit vindictive, wanting revenge, and he had the urge to control God by telling Him what to do! So all of these elements of unrighteous anger are demonstrated to a certain extent in this part of the passage (although David does go on to acknowledge that God is trustworthy and praises him: 'I'm proud to praise God!' (v10, *The Message*)).

We know that David was a man after God's heart, even though he struggled at times, doing and saying things he shouldn't. Interestingly, he felt safe enough to rant in front of God, but also acknowledged God's sovereignty, turning his anger into praise to God. Whatever he was doing, God still loved him and it's great that when we read this it causes us to remember that although none of us is perfect, God still loves us, too. This fills us with hope.

So what else does the Bible say about unrighteous anger? Well, take a look at Proverbs 29:11, 'Fools vent their anger, but the wise quietly hold it back' (NLT). So when there is a conflict situation it is not healthy for our anger to come out in an uncontrolled way. It is more important to try to create the right sort of environment for finding a solution (which we will look at in more detail later). As Proverbs 15:1 says, 'A gentle answer turns away wrath, but a harsh word stirs up anger.' Just the simple approach of speaking quietly is far more likely to reduce conflict to a more manageable situation.

It was Aristotle who said: 'Anyone can be angry. That is easy. But to be angry with the right person to the right degree, at the right time, for the right purpose, and in the right way – that is not ... easy.'[8]

Interesting quotation isn't it? It's so true, and part of handling conflict is knowing when it is appropriate for anger to be brought into the situation. As the seventeenth-century reverend William Secker said, 'He that would be angry and not sin must be angry at nothing but sin.'[9] That's another great quote to ponder!

Secker's challenge to us is to be angry at the sin rather than the sinner; to be angry with the behaviour, not the individual person, who is just as loved by God and worthy of His grace and forgiveness as we are.

How conflict and anger affect our physical functioning

We have looked at what righteous anger is, and is not, now it's important to look at how anger affects our physical bodies.

The physiology of anger – the fight or flight response

The phrase 'fight or flight' refers to an entirely automatic response that our bodies make when we face a situation of potential danger (which conflict and stress can be). This is also called the 'alarm reaction'. It is an unconscious biochemical reaction to a threat. Imagine the physical feelings associated with being in a 'near miss' in a car, and think about how similar the feelings are when we are faced with a personal threat such as rejection. These feelings are how God has created us physiologically in order to respond to, and cope with, danger.

What actually happens is that the brain picks up a potential crisis and prepares the body to either fight the perceived threat or run away from it (take flight). This is obviously essential in life-threatening situations when, perhaps, oncoming traffic suddenly swerves towards you. When our self-preservation instinct kicks in, it will ensure that we respond more quickly in order to protect ourselves from danger. However, when we experience a threat to our self-image or someone insists on their own way, we can become very angry because the 'fight or flight' response is to the threat to our personhood. Our bodies can't automatically differentiate between an objective and a subjective threat.

The next diagram gives a very simplified overview of what happens to our bodies when we experience an emotional arousal of anger during a conflict situation.

The Autonomic Nervous System 'fight or flight' response

Eyes and/or ears sense a threat

and/or

Distorted thoughts feed the mind that there is a threat

The brain goes on red alert and sends messages down to the adrenalin glands (on top of kidneys)

These glands then release adrenalin into our bloodstream

Blood vessels carry the adrenalin around the body

The muscles in the body have more energy to be released for fight or flight

The rapid release of adrenalin affects the physiology of our bodies, bringing about the following changes: heart rate and blood pressure increase; respiration deepens and becomes quicker; pupils dilate; mouth goes dry and hands can go clammy; neck and shoulder muscles tense, and blood is diverted from the skin, stomach and intestines to the heart, central nervous system and muscles because the body is preparing for action. All this can cause the digestive system to close down; some people get stomach upsets in response to anger and because our bladder muscles relax we may want to go the toilet more frequently. It can also be difficult to focus on small tasks because our brain is focused on the bigger picture of the source of the threat. That is why it is so difficult to concentrate on other matters when our bodies are stressed.

However, our body's natural reaction to stress is not so appropriate for today's everyday strains and conflicts, which means the pressure can build up without an outlet. People's anger can become out of control due to all the adrenalin, with its resulting energy, being pumped around the body. In a conflict situation, of course, this can cause a violent response – verbally or even physically. So it's really important for us to be able to recognise when our emotions are aroused and when the energy that accompanies anger is becoming out of control in order to remove ourselves. It's also important to be able to identify it within someone else so we can stay out of their way. Recognising the signs of adrenalin racing around our body can be a cue that a conflict is brewing. Things can spiral very quickly from a quiet disagreement to a big conflict situation, so it is important to allow those involved to calm it down, protect themselves and recognise that it's not the time to start trying to resolve it. Conflict resolution will be addressed in the last chapter.

There are many passive and active forms of anger that can bubble away under the surface and then explode (see Appendix 3).

Factors that can feed frustration, anger and general low mood
Many life issues can affect our mood. When we are stressed, tired or have low energy levels we are far more vulnerable to having a short fuse. Both Chris and Claire know they have caused a conflict purely because they were overtired or stressed with the never-ending demands of being a parent! Sometimes when tired we don't have the same resources to cope with difficult or annoying situations. So what are the factors that cause us to feel low or angry more quickly than we would normally?

State of health – we all know how hard it is to respond without snapping when we are feeling really ill. As already mentioned, we are whole people and when we suffer physical, emotional or mental pain, this has the propensity to affect our mood, which can cause depressive symptoms. In his book, *The Psychology of Melancholy*, Matthew Ostow writes, 'Depression, at every phase of its development, includes a component of anger, whether visible or invisible, whether conscious or unconscious.'[10] And we know when anger is around we are far more likely to become embroiled in a conflict situation.

Exercise – this is an interesting one. While a lack of exercise for some people can cause frustration and anger, an aggressive form of exercise can cause others to feel angrier in their everyday life too. It has been thought, for example, that the aggressive training undertaken by the Forces is purposeful in that it prepares the service men and women for conflict. But some find they are unable to reduce their heightened arousal and, even when away from war zones, they may become angry and cause conflict.

Also, if a person is naturally bent towards wanting to win all the time, then playing a team game like football could increase their anger levels if they aren't able to score a goal! We are all individual and different types of exercise may or may not frustrate us.

Nutrition – the importance of eating a well-balanced diet is well recognised, but how many of us actually pay attention to the fact that eating well makes us feel better too? For instance, it is a well accepted fact that caffeine can affect our mood. Most of us know how irritable we become when we lose our appetite due to stress!

Consumption of certain drugs – recreational drugs such as heroin and cocaine can lead to angry outbursts. Some people have experienced heightened anger when on medical drugs such as steroids – this anger is better known as 'roid rage'.[11]

Alcohol – Chris has found in her work that some people become more belligerent and difficult when they drink quite a lot of alcohol, causing a lot more conflict.

Quality of sleep – lack of good-quality sleep will cause tiredness, which, as already mentioned, has a knock-on effect to our mood. When our bodies are carrying a lot of tension, or our minds can't switch off, we can't sleep and thus we become even more tired – leading to more 'flare ups'.

Life stresses – both Chris and Claire find that the everyday stresses of life, such as demanding work and home schedules, cause their fuses to get shorter. A fast pace of life, a shortage of jobs or fear of redundancy can affect our inner world, leaving us frustrated and tense with anxiety.

Social factors – because we live in a fast-moving society that demands more and more from us, our energy and emotional resources are being stretched to their limit so we become irritable more quickly and hit out at others. The fact that we are a more mobile society also means that work can take us away from our family support structures, leaving us exposed to coping by ourselves. The lack of social support can feed a low mood, thus we become more frustrated and again end up with a short fuse in a conflict situation.

ACTIVITY
Looking at the factors cited above, what would you say influences your mood most? How does that affect your anger and the way you behave towards others?

Skills to keep our emotional arousal levels down
As already mentioned, it's important that we recognise the increasing energy in the emotion of anger – before it has 'donned its boxing gloves and armour' and causes a conflict.

1. Learning the techniques of deep breathing
Slow, controlled breathing is a great aid to relaxation. If we can catch the anger by *breathing* ourselves into a calmer state, we can then deal with the issues rather than our emotions.

Calming ourselves down
- Find a comfy chair and sit upright.
- Be aware of the chair taking your weight and note the different sensations in your body, ie how your back feels against the chair; note the sensation in your feet resting on the floor.
- Note any noises that may be around.
- What is going through your mind? Try putting your thoughts in an imaginary box and place that box on an imaginary shelf. Think of peace and calm.

- Be aware of your breathing and try to slow it down.
- Note the difference between the in-breath (inhalation) and the out-breaths (exhalation).
- Continue in this rhythm and count how long your in-breath takes and how long your out-breath takes.
- Now make the out-breath longer than the in-breath. For example, if the in-breath is three counts, make the out-breath five counts (2/5 or 4/6, 5/8, etc. It's important to make the out-breaths longer than the in-breaths because this dampens down the arousal response.)
- Try breathing out using a deep sigh, rather like a balloon deflating.
- Continue to breathe deeply for a few minutes and note how much more relaxed and calm your body is.
- Now as you breathe out, say the word 'peace' very slowly, letting a peaceful scene such as water, or a country scene come into your mind.

2. The importance of regular relaxation

Having noted that in any conflict situation our bodies become tense, it follows that if we are able to relax our bodies the tension will lessen and to some degree our anger will disperse. We all have our own way of relaxing: reading a good book; doing sudoku; listening to music; going for a walk, soaking in a hot bubble bath and so on.[12]

3. Living a healthy lifestyle

We live in society that is so hurried it constantly drives us forward in the fast lane. Unfortunately not many of us have time to stop or slow down, which would help re-energise and refresh us to live in a calmer way. Adopting a healthy lifestyle will include a balance of stillness, rest, busyness, exercise, challenges, creativity, fun and laughter with others – a balance of all will help keep stress at bay. A healthy lifestyle will help us to have emotional and mental wellbeing, which will, in turn, give us a stronger ability to cope with the stresses and strains of life.[13]

Unhealthy roots and unhealthy fruits: the conflict tree

As we've seen previously, a lot of unresolved conflict stays that way because the individuals involved are stuck at the level of self-interest. At least one of them is saying, 'I want to do this, it's all about me.' The root of that could be because they are feeling a bit insecure, or worthless. There are many roots for such thoughts, which grow up into things like idealistic demands: 'you should do this or that because I'm telling you to', or a lack of acceptance of other people's attitudes and values. As a result the tree produces unhealthy fruits. To take this analogy further, when the fruit is picked by another (ie there is an interaction – or transaction), then conflict very often occurs.

Take a look at Appendix 4. This shows an example of the sort of roots we can have in our lives and how they can affect every branch and twig. What unhealthy fruit can you think of? Perhaps greed, hatred, power, avoidance, jealousy, indecisiveness, disunity and so on. This picture is trying to illustrate in a simple way how such selfish roots grow unhealthy branches and how these in turn grow unhealthy fruits on the tree that creates an environment for conflict.

So, let's think about a specific example.

A type of unhealthy fruit that can grow out of such a self-centred tree could be jealousy. A root of insecurity can grow a lack of trust and this in turn can grow into unhealthy fruit. Jealousy in any close relationship can wrongly perceive that one's partner's attention and affection are being displaced upon another. Such suspicion can give rise to uncontrollable anger, then the volcano erupts into conflict. 'Anger is cruel and fury overwhelming, but who can stand before jealousy?' (Prov. 27:4).

Let's take another example, again starting at the roots. How would a lack of self-esteem affect a person? The roots of worthlessness and insecurity will result in pain that causes certain coping mechanisms to be adopted. These may be unrealistic demands and preferences ('I've got to have it like this') or lack of acceptance ('I can't accept myself so I can't possibly accept you'). The resulting behaviour could be that the person ends up hardened and gets quite abusive, thereby igniting conflict.

These are just a couple of simple examples of what can happen when our lives grow from corrupt roots. If we haven't got a firm base and security through meeting our deep needs in God, the negative comes up through the roots and through the trunk, bearing fruit that can give rise to conflict. Of course we all come up against other people who have diseased roots, too. And there are lots of lovely people out there who are not rooted in God, they don't even believe in God, but who actually have great value systems anyway. But none of us is perfect and, whether we are believers or not, there will be at least some roots that need work because they are self-centred.

ACTIVITY

Think of an occasion when you felt angry.

- What kind of anger was it? Look at Appendix 4 to identify your kind of anger.
- Play with creating and drawing your own conflict tree, identifying your roots and fruits.

REFLECTION

As we have been looking at some of the factors that are behind most conflicts, think about yourself and the way you respond to people. Do you have a tendency to look to others to fulfil your needs? Do you go into relationships with unconscious goals you want to see fulfilled?

PRAYER

Thank You Lord that You, and You alone, are the source of our contentment. Help me to ensure I always come to You to have my inner needs met rather than looking at others to fulfil them for me. And help me to remember who I am in You, and how much You love me. Amen.

CHAPTER 3

FACTORS THAT CHARACTERISE CONFLICTS: OUR MINDS

THOUGHTS AND PERCEPTIONS

Many conflicts are the resulting damage of our thoughts, perceptions and misperceptions. When we are involved in conflict we may disagree on how something is perceived and, unless we first clarify how each of us is actually viewing the situation, the conflict may not be resolved.

Faulty thinking has such a huge affect on conflict. Indeed, Ephesians 4:17 calls it futile: 'So I tell you this, and insist on it in the Lord, that you must no longer live as the Gentiles do, in the futility of their thinking.'

The Bible has a great example of the difference perceptions can make. In Numbers 13:17–33 we can read the well known story of the twelve spying out the land of Canaan to see 'what the land is like and whether the people who live there are strong or weak, few or many' (v18). Out of the twelve, only two of them had anything positive to say. Listen to what Caleb's report was, 'We should go up and take possession of the land, for we can certainly do it' (v30). In stark contrast to this is the response of the majority of the spies. Their fear gave them a totally different perception, 'We can't attack those people; they are stronger than we are' (v31) and 'We seemed like grasshoppers in our own eyes, and we looked the same to them' (v33). They all visited the same land, but they had two very different perceptions of it.

Interestingly, out of those twelve (who were all leaders in their own right, by the way), the ten who had been negative allowed their fear to give rise to unbelief and they ended up forfeiting entry to the promised land. Joshua and Caleb, on the other hand, the only two who had been full of faith and positivity, did get to enter it. What a difference perception can make!

To use an up-to-date example, imagine yourself at the top of a big dipper. What is going through your mind? Terror? Slight panic? Oh I'm looking forward to this! Oh this is exciting! Ooh, wonderful! Oh no, my goodness I'm going to be sick any moment now! I'm terrified! All those responses are facing the exact same thing, but they reveal different perceptions. So when you are working with conflict it can be helpful to think of it as the same thing viewed from different sides. The challenge is to try to understand each other's viewpoints in order to be able to resolve the conflict and gain reconciliation.

Of course, how we view the triggers and their meaning to us will determine the intensity of our anger and to what degree we get stuck in a conflict situation. Having differences doesn't inevitably mean conflict. It is how we handle these differences that determine that. If we take a hostile view of them, then they will become a trigger for anger. If we view tension tolerantly, in a gracious godly way, it doesn't have to be destructive. Tension becomes conflict when the people involved can no longer deal with it constructively. In those moments we lose sight of God!

Distorted self-perceptions

When we base our identity on what others think of us and the way they treat us this becomes a breeding ground for damaging conflict. That is why it is so important that we know who we are in Christ.

We can take this even further, and allow the way a person or group (supposedly) perceives us to cause problems.

Some conflicts arise out of what individuals perceive as a threat. A threat is a person or situation that may cause possible danger; sometimes people see threats where they do not exist and the unfortunate result is conflict.

ACTIVITY

Try and identify how different the thoughts may be in the following scenarios:

1. Why does one person in the office always agree with his boss (who is never wrong!) even when he knows his boss is not right, and another will have a stand up conflict over the issues?

2. Why does one woman get angry and have a row with her husband every time he comes home late from work, while another doesn't?

3. Why does one person get angry when her boss at work constructively criticises the team but her teammate doesn't?

4. Why does a mother hit the ceiling when her daughter comes in late and has a row with her, while another mother doesn't?

As this exercise will hopefully have revealed to you, it isn't the trigger itself that produces the anger, but what goes through a person's mind.

VALUES

A value is something we consider as significantly important to us, such as honesty or staying true to our promises (ie faithfulness in marriage). In any conflict it is important to tease out the differences between values and principles, ethical and moral beliefs and preferences. Resolving conflicts that are caused by people's values will, at times, involve accepting differences. There are always going to be different values – for example, you will no doubt live by your Christian values but another person in the workplace won't because they don't hold the same beliefs as you. They may not understand your viewpoint precisely because of your differing value systems, and it is important to bear that in mind as it can help you to treat them with more respect. However, there may be some differences that you don't feel you can resolve.

Chris has counselled quite a number of couples in which the husband has had an affair. The couple's differing beliefs and values may come to light as the situation is explored. Perhaps the husband perceives his affair as being acceptable because he blames his wife that she doesn't want any intimacy or sex, whereas she is left devastated seeing his affair as an utter betrayal of trust. This clash of different value systems causes much hurt, with resulting conflict.

BELIEFS

We all have beliefs about ourselves, others' and the world around us, which will feed into how we behave. For example, a driven over-achiever is more vulnerable to conflict patterns of behaviour. Why? Because they may fall into the following traps:

- Believing that they should do everything perfectly.
- Believing that everyone around them should have the same standards.
- Believing that their many and notable accomplishments give them a certain status.
- Failing to acknowledge that their status is self-generated, rather than given.
- Seeking self-generated acceptance and affirmation, which gets them hooked into going round and round a circle, burning out badly in the process.

We all hold deep beliefs about who we are and how we operate. A healthy belief about self may be 'I'm likeable' whereas an unhealthy belief may be 'I'm worthless'. We also have beliefs about how we are doing in life, 'My best isn't good enough', 'I'm stupid, whatever I do is not right' or 'I'm a total failure'. Arising from our core beliefs are automatic thoughts and assumptions.

The negative beliefs that we have about ourselves trigger this process, creating negative automatic thoughts (NATs). Note that they are automatic. We don't have any control over them coming into our heads, but we do have control of whether we entertain or dismiss them. For example, when Chris is at one of her lowest moments the belief that crops up about herself is 'I'm inadequate'. Deep in her heart, rationally she knows she is not inadequate professionally or in her personal life, but if she's stressed or exhausted then that's the belief that raises its ugly head. Then from this thought an assumption could arise that says something like: 'If I always please people, then I won't feel so inadequate!'

Each one of us needs to recognise that we have a deep belief system about ourselves that comes into play in our lives. For instance, if you believe that your many and notable accomplishments give you a certain status then your belief system could be about gaining a sense of significance. Failing to acknowledge the trap of seeking self-generated acceptance and affirmation, rather than seeking to meet your needs in God, could turn you into an approval junkie. Getting such approval will provide you with a buzz, but when you come across someone you don't think is affirming you there's going to be a conflict because inside you are thinking 'how dare you not approve of me'. (This is a blocked goal.) That would be the belief on which your sense of self is based – and the result when you come across someone who challenges that.

Let's look at a few examples of a belief system and how they can come into play within a conflict situation:

If my belief is: 'I am stupid'
NAT – I am silly.
Assumption – if I try and do that, then I will get it all wrong.
In a conflict situation – I'm an avoider.

If my belief is: 'I'm no good'
NAT – I can't get anything right.
Assumption – but if I tell them what to do, then I will feel better about myself.
In a conflict situation – I dominate.

If my belief is: 'I'm unloveable'
NAT – no one likes me or needs me.

70

Assumption – therefore, if I try and sort this out, then people will like me.
In a conflict situation – I am a people pleaser.

If my belief is: 'I'm hopeless'
NAT – I need everyone's accolade so I must sort this now in order to achieve and prove to myself I am not hopeless.
Assumption – if I try and sort this out, then people will affirm me.
In a conflict situation – I am a quick fixer or bargainer.

If my belief is: 'I am worthless'
NAT – I am nothing.
Assumption – if I give in to this demand, then people will accept me.
In a conflict situation – I play the game 'peace at any price'.

If my belief is: 'I am insecure'
NAT – I must be in control.
Assumption – if I am in control then I will feel better.
In a conflict situation – I win, you lose.

Let's ponder one of those further. The belief that 'I'm worthless, I'm nothing' results in the thought that 'if I give in to another person's demand I'll be affirmed' and because of a desperate need for acceptance 'I feel that it will, at least, give me a bit of something, even if it isn't really the result I want'. So many people are like this; because they feel so low about themselves they'd rather give in and get some acceptance than actually learn to handle their conflicts. They need to work on building their self-worth before they are able to deal with conflict situations.

Another thing about assumptions is that we have a tendency to assume that others will react in the same way as us and feel the same way as us, but of course that's not true. We are all built differently and therefore will react differently. We need to be aware of that and make allowances for that too.

ACTIVITY

Try to identify one of your negative core beliefs. Then try to listen to what you are saying about that and the subsequent assumption. An assumption tends to have the following wording: If _____then _____ . Go back to the examples above and observe this pattern. Fill in the activity below and reflect on what you can learn from this.

Belief about self_____
NATs_____
_____
Assumption _____
_____
In a conflict situation I am _____
_____

POWER AND HOW WE CHOOSE TO BEHAVE

Another one of the five areas of human functioning that we are looking at in this book is how we engage our will and choose to behave. In other words, it is about how we use our power of choice (ie the volitional area of functioning). As we explored earlier, many people see power as dominance, exerting control, competing to win or gaining advantage. How we define power and use it ourselves will greatly impact our relationships and the way we manage the inevitable conflicts. However, power doesn't always have to be a negative force. A healthy approach to power is choosing to act effectively within the areas we have the ability to influence.

Many people become so stuck in their relationship style that they don't realise that God has given them a mind and will and that there may be other options of interaction that they can choose. Chris has great fun role playing with clients as they learn to use different skills that they had no idea could be appropriate to use in a potential conflict situation.

> Bethany last visited her mother in Germany two years ago. Every hour of every day her mum crammed in activities for them both, and when Bethany said she just wanted a day to 'chill' her mother nearly went ballistic. She had made plans for the day and accused Bethany of not being grateful and of being selfish - you can imagine the conflict!

Now Bethany, who was recovering from an operation, told Chris she was really anxious about visiting her mum back in Germany for another holiday. She was concerned that she wasn't well enough to keep up with her mum's speed and expectations, and was fearful that there would be an inevitable conflict about this. In the counselling room, through role play, Chris and Bethany explored the possible scenarios and the reactions she could choose in order to address this potential conflict. Bethany ended up sending her mother an email before her holidays, saying that she wasn't well enough to do the usual activities. She recognised that this would disappoint her mother and stated that she would only be well enough to do an activity every afternoon and no more. Her mother accepted this and the holiday was a great success.

How our inner world can infect itself

How God has created us is amazing; our inner world of ideas, thoughts, beliefs and perceptions all interact together to influence how we choose to engage our will and subsequently choose to behave. Each part of our inner world 'infects' the other in either a positive or negative way. If we are feeling tense with unhealthy negative thoughts, then the impact can create a ripe environment for conflict. We can start noticing annoying things about another person (that possibly don't bother us normally) and this starts to get under our skin. Our tolerance level drops and their behaviour winds us up, which leaves us focusing even more on their behaviour and in turn annoys us further. Our perception of that person begins to change and instead of lovingly accepting their annoying habits, we begin to tell them to stop it! We try to use our power to stop something that is quite innocent, but because we can't handle it we don't pause and think of what constructive choices we could make in the situation. Instead, we respond with bitterness and lash out. Yes, we allow another conflict situation over something pretty innocent and innocuous.

ACTIVITY

'A gentle answer turns away wrath, but a harsh word stirs up anger' (Prov. 15:1).

Bring to mind a time when you were angry. Now try to think of a gentle answer to replace the one you gave.

REFLECTION

Take some time to prayerfully consider whether you have any areas in your mind in which you need to do battle. Remember that God tells us to 'take captive every thought to make it obedient to Christ' (2 Cor. 10:5). Are there any thoughts, beliefs or values that you need to bring back into line with God's Word? Ask Him to help you do that now.

PRAYER

Thank You Lord that we have a choice about how we behave – and how we think. Help me to be guided more by Your Spirit and to take a step back and consider possible alternatives to my usual thoughts and actions. Open my eyes to see things, and people, the way that You do; give me a new perspective on the world around me and my inner being.

CHAPTER FOUR

HANDLING CONFLICT WELL

BE A PEACEMAKER, NOT A CONFLICT CREATOR

First and foremost, when entering conflict of any kind we need to remind ourselves that, as Christians, we are called to be peacemakers. This does not mean that we should be looking for peace at any price in any conflict situation, as that gives those who naturally avoid conflict an excuse – and could also mean we are unjustly treated. What it does mean is that we actively and creatively work towards peace and order in the situation.

Jesus said, 'Blessed are the peacemakers, for they will be called children of God' (Matt 5:9). The same passage in *The Message* is really interesting: 'You're blessed when you can show people how to cooperate instead of compete or fight. That's when you discover who you really are, and your place in God's family.'

Those words are really great, especially when we are thinking about conflict. Jesus was very direct when speaking about relationships, warning us to have nothing to do with any forms of biased criticism, condemnation and judgment of others.

A critical attitude can often come from jealousy, a sense of inferiority or egocentricity.

Sometimes criticism is said under the guise of love, 'I am saying this in love', yet it feels more like anger than any motivation of love. Often the fault we find in others is simply a projection of our own faults (ie we cover up faults that we are conscious of within our own selves but are very unforgiving towards others who have them).

Do not judge

Matthew 7:1 is very direct and simple on this matter, 'Do not judge, or you too will be judged.' One reason people harbour grudges is that they are only aware of some of the facts that surround the conflict. Sometimes to know all is to forgive all. Selwyn Hughes once said that in the early years of his life he would go about judging others and trying to run God's universe for Him, but he broke down physically as a result. A wise friend advised him: 'Selwyn, stop trying to run the world and act the part of God.'[14] Only God knows the motives that prompt people to act the way they do. Our task is to love everybody – and leave the judgment to God.

Chris once heard a preacher say that when we are in the prosecutor's stand we cannot be in the witness box. That means that if we are denouncing others we are not announcing Jesus. That's certainly something to think about …

RESPONDING WITH GRACE AND FORGIVENESS

When dealing with any conflict we are aware that the anger involved can easily turn into resentment, which can then turn into bitterness. We can all have a tendency to react like this, so it's really important to learn to handle conflict, and the people involved, with grace and forgiveness. (Later, we will be looking further at ensuring the pain and hurt involved is dealt with before trying to forgive.)

We must remind ourselves that Jesus said: 'For if you forgive other people when they sin against you, your heavenly Father will also forgive you' (Matt. 6:14). As God has forgiven us, it's important we forgive. We cannot live happily and healthily in our bodies if we have resentment in our hearts.

Why do we want to hang on to resentment and bitterness even though we know we have been forgiven? The answer, in part, is because of a 'touchy', un-surrendered self. We believe we have a right to feel the way that we do. When we hold on to resentment it is because there is a part of our self that is un-surrendered to the will of God. If we were living in complete surrender we could simply let go of the conflict rather than allowing resentment to build up against the person involved. So when trying to deal with this, go beyond the root cause of resentment and look for the un-surrendered self.

One way of learning to let go of resentment is by cultivating the following habit: every time you think of someone who has injured you, turn your thoughts to pray for them. God asked us to love our enemies, and to pray for those who hurt us (Matt. 5:44). Indeed the first words from the cross were, 'Father, forgive them, for they do not know what they are doing' (Luke 23:34). Wow, those are such moving words from Jesus. Your immediate response may be, 'I can't forgive to that extent', but remember that Jesus lives in you and His love can flow through you. The challenge here is to learn to surrender our problems and feelings into His hands and He will, slowly over time, enable us to forgive the deepest hurt.

RECONCILIATION

2 Corinthians 5:18 says that, 'God … reconciled us to himself through Christ and gave us the ministry of reconciliation.' *The Message* puts it like this: 'God … settled the relationship between us and him, and then called us to settle our relationships with each other … We're Christ's representatives. God uses us to persuade men and women to drop their differences and enter into God's work of making things right between them' (vv18–19).

God made possible the relationship between us and Him and then called us to resolve our relationship with each other. *The Message* version of the above verses highlights the fact that God uses us to persuade men and women to drop their differences. How many times have we mentioned already that it is differences that cause conflict? And, bringing God's Word into it, He wants us to put those differences aside in order to promote unity and reconciliation. It's interesting to note that a lot of the teaching on conflict resolution is based on Scripture …

The Greek word Paul uses for reconciliation in this passage is *katalasso*, which means 'to change mutually' or 'to change completely'. In other words, reconciliation has as its goal a change in the nature of relationships, and few changes take place without some degree of pain – no pain, no gain!

The *Compact Oxford English Dictionary* helps us to understand the link between effort and change: the verb 'to reconcile' suggests: 'to make friendly after an estrangement; settle (a quarrel); harmonise; make compatible.'[15]

If we are to be reconcilers it's all about pursuing:
- harmony rather than adding to friction
- peace and unity while withdrawing from dissension
- a solution rather than contribute to conflict.

In the words of Francis of Assisi, let our prayer be:

> Lord, make me an instrument of your peace;
> where there is hatred, let me sow love;
> where there is injury, pardon;
> where there is doubt, faith;
> where there is despair, hope;
> where there is darkness, light;
> and where there is sadness, joy.
> O Divine Master,
> grant that I may not so much seek
> to be consoled as to console;
> to be understood, as to understand;
> to be loved, as to love;
> for it is in giving that we receive,
> it is in pardoning that we are pardoned,
> and it is in dying that we are born to Eternal Life.
> Amen.

Those very words drip with the right attitude don't they?

If ever there was a world leader who demonstrated love and forgiveness, it was Nelson Mandela. As we write this book, news has just broken that he has died. His story illustrates how he brought about reconciliation between the division of races in South Africa. At great personal cost he fought against the evils of apartheid. Having survived twenty-seven years of oppression in prison and hard labour in a limestone quarry, he emerged to preach reconciliation. 'He showed that bitter conflict could be resolved with dialogue' (*The Times*, Friday 6 December 2013). The world has honoured him as an amazing, humble and forgiving man who had no hint of bitterness after suffering such hardship and unfairness. What a challenge to us when we face conflict.

Letting go of pain

Although forgiveness and repentance are crucial to the resolution of conflict, it's important that repentance is accompanied by healing before reconciliation can take place. Reconciliation is not saying: 'OK, we'll all be friends now – just forget all that has happened – let's leave it behind.' In its desire to see reconciliation occur the Church can sometimes push for forgiveness too quickly rather than allowing people time to get in touch with their hurt and pain in order for the forgiveness to flow out of a place of healing.

Chris has had the pleasure of meeting the Christian psychiatrist Dr Rhiannon Lloyd from Wales several times and hearing something of her story. From a civil war in Burundi from 1993–2005, conflict spilled over into neighbouring Rwanda in 1994 when a Hutu-led genocide was perpetrated, resulting in Tutsis and Hutus slaughtering one another. Throughout the course of 100 days, between 800,000 and one million Tutsis and Hutus were massacred in this genocide. Rhiannon, with her colleague Kristine Bresser, went to Rwanda in the aftermath of this genocide to try and bring reconciliation between the sides. She invited both Tutsi and Hutu Christian leaders to a three-day seminar. Now just pause for a moment and imagine what that would have meant. Sitting in the same room with someone, even a neighbour, who had hacked to death a family member – how emotionally charged that room would have been! Right at the beginning, both Rhiannon and Kristine decided that it would be unhelpful to even talk about 'forgiveness' until later;

that they should do so only when the participants' hearts had been softened with God's love. They recognised that reconciliation is not about smoothing over all the pain and hurt that has occurred, but it is a deeper process.

On the first day the participants were invited to recall what they had seen, heard and experienced during the war and then think about God and where He was in the trauma. Then Rhiannon posed three questions: 'Is everything that happens in the world the will of God? If God is all loving why does He permit the innocent to suffer? And if God is all powerful why doesn't He intervene and stop all evil people doing evil things?'

As the groups were exploring these questions, Rhiannon explained that God's heart had been full of grief at what He'd witnessed in the genocide, with individuals pursuing the inclinations of their own hearts. She tried to tune in to the emotionally charged atmosphere in the room by saying that God really cares for every individual in Rwanda; that He weeps with them and all that happened. Slowly hope was sown as it dawned on them that the sovereign God cared for each of them individually and that He could redeem every human tragedy.

Hearts were softened as Rhiannon went on to talk about God's love and the power of the cross. She asked them to think about their worst experience in the genocide, to write it down and then share this personal experience within the group. With some finding this emotionally and culturally difficult, Rhiannon gently guided their thoughts towards how God felt about their story.

Gradually Tutsis and Hutus began to share their experiences one with another. They were also encouraged to be honest with God and tell Him about the emotional pain arising from their experiences. Slowly they began to weep and pray together.

On the second day, Rhiannon carried a great big rough wooden cross into the room and a hammer with a pile of nails. She invited them to take their pieces of paper with their painful stories, and nail them onto the cross. Hearing the hammering of the nails and then the songs of praise on their lips as they returned to their seats, renewed and free in their spirits, was awe inspiring.

Up until this point, the words 'forgiveness and reconciliation' still hadn't been mentioned. On the last day they were invited to share what God had been doing in their hearts. One after another, there were joyous testimonies of God's saving grace. Their hearts had been changed and a new love replaced the hatred they had hitherto felt, enabling forgiveness to flow.

Rhiannon herself commented that: 'before wounded people can be expected to forgive, a place must be provided where they can face the pain, talk about their wounds and experience God's healing touch. *Then* from the wellspring of their hearts the grace to forgive will flow like a cleansing stream.'[16]

Healing cannot be hurried – it is so beautiful to read about what happened within those three days, but sometimes pain can take years to heal fully.

We felt we needed to include a story like that to show the importance of not rushing ahead to talk about forgiveness and reconciliation. So often, when counselling others in conflict situations, we can be quick to talk about the need to forgive but don't recognise that the person right in front of us is sitting in a huge pile of hurt. In such instances we are simply trying to put a sticky plaster over the mess rather than allowing them to get in touch with their deep pain in order for God to bring healing.

The need for allowing such space is well known now in the psychology field. Chris went to an excellent secular psychology conference that was covering the issue of forgiveness and was struck by the fact that everyone there agreed that we need to help people get in touch with the deep pain and hurt first by unravelling and detoxifying it. This happens by understanding the experience and the people involved; only then can they untangle the conflict and perhaps come to the place of forgiveness.

As Christians it is vital that we recognise the need to get in touch with our own deep hurt, and bring that to God to deal with, before we can actually extend forgiveness to the person who has hurt us so much. It's so important that we walk the way of the cross when dealing with hurt, forgiveness and reconciliation.

ACTIVITY

We are very aware that telling a story about pain and reconciliation may have brought up a lot of pain for those still facing difficult conflict situations. You may be struggling even with the concept of sitting in the same room as the person who has hurt you, and so we want to give you a bit of time and space if you need it here.

Realise that you are loved and accepted in the place you are at. If you're not ready to forgive, God already knows that so simply open up to Him by saying: 'Lord I want my heart to be willing to forgive when it is appropriate but for now help me to get in touch with the pain and bring it to you.'

Now, in a time of quietness, allow the pain to surface – as much as you are able to. Remind yourself that God is weeping with you in that place. He is hurting with you and He cries with you. He sees how you've been trodden on through the words that have been spoken to you and it's pierced His heart as well. He can feel it with you. And He senses the unfairness of it all.

He is saying to you: 'You can trust me with your pain and your hurt. I will carry that for you; it is not yours to carry.' As much as you are able, try to give Him the pain. Imagine it flowing into His heart – or pour it out at the foot of the cross (choose whichever image is more helpful for you). Now accept that He's pouring in comfort where you're hurting. He's pouring in soothing oil, cleansing and healing you, touching your spirit and saying, 'You're worth everything to me. You are mine. I know you by name; you're the apple of my eye. Though you may walk through the waters of conflict sometimes, you will not be overwhelmed for I am with you.'

Just sit for a little while longer to see whatever else God wants to do for you or say to you before moving on.

Letting go of the desire for reconciliation

Sometimes it will be the case that one person wants reconciliation but the other person simply doesn't. That can be a very painful place to be, but we also have to accept it. We can't be God. We can only do so much and learn to leave the situation in God's hands. We can carry on praying and loving the other person but if they choose to reject the relationship we can't do anything more about it.

Chris has worked with a Christian teenage girl, Kate, whose story illustrates the importance of letting go. She had a very traumatic childhood with her dad, experiencing abuse of nearly every kind. When she first went to see Chris, Kate was still hoping for reconciliation with her dad. The teenager longed for him to accept her and love her as his daughter, so she kept trying to do everything in her power to have a relationship – buying him birthday cards that were ignored, and popping round to the house only to have the curtains drawn in her face. This repeated hurt of rejection caused her to self-harm. While she longs for reconciliation, sadly there will be none unless he also wants to have a relationship with his daughter. At the moment, it is obvious that he doesn't. So part of Chris's counselling work has been helping this young lady process all the hurt and disappointment, and come to realise that her relationship with her dad may never go any further. At first this was a huge loss and it was painful for her to come to terms with it. Having worked through much of her agony over a number of years, this lady, who is now in her twenties, is accepting that her relationship with her dad will never be different unless he chooses to change. Consequently she is feeling much better in herself. The inner conflict of self-hate she experienced is improving and she has stopped self-harming.

As this sad story reveals, you cannot resolve a conflict if one party is absolutely adamant they don't want to. You can only try to be reasonable and do everything you can. One of the important things about trying to resolve conflict creatively is recognising that it may not be fully resolved. You may have to learn to live with that frustration and find your sense of worth and security in God within that difficult place, knowing that you will only ever find true peace in Him.

FORGIVENESS AND ACCEPTANCE OF SELF

In our internal world, we can sometimes find that different parts of ourselves are in conflict with other parts and this will obviously have an impact on the way we respond to others. This can come out in various forms:

Self-attacking

This arises from an inner conflict when we feel frustrated with ourselves and believe the lie that 'I am flawed'. Consequently we attack ourselves for not being good enough, telling ourselves lies such as: 'I'm hopeless and will never amount to anything.'

This self-attacking part of ourselves can cause us to feel bad about what we have or have not done and we can end up crushed with the heaviness of guilt. Guilt always wants us to punish ourselves, so we may get drawn into conflict situations, sabotaging opportunities and destroying relationships. Or, we may attack ourselves by saying, 'I deserve to be punished' and turn to self-harm.

Self-criticism

This inner voice attacks us by constantly criticising us for not doing things well enough. 'I should do everything perfectly.' 'I shouldn't have said that.' 'I need to improve and do better.' Therefore we often drive ourselves, to try harder and in the long run become more stressed with ourselves and this short fuse can cause conflict. Imagine the heavy cloak around us when we are constantly putting ourselves down. We can sometimes belittle ourselves in a way that we would never do with our friends.

Self-hatred/self-disgust

This voice attacks our fundamental self-worth. It is deeply shaming and tells us that who we are is bad – that we shouldn't even exist. 'I hate myself.' This inner conflict arises from a belief of unworthiness: 'I must hurt/destroy myself.'

> Annie was feeling very low and depressed. Her parents had always been hypercritical of her. She could never please them and she was never good enough for them. Something was always wrong about her. Consequently they used to hit her. As a result Annie was full of self-hatred and was always criticising herself, whatever she did.

In exploring these issues, it came to light that Annie was not able to accept herself because she thought it was all her fault that her parents beat her. Her assumption was that 'if I was different, then my parents wouldn't have hit me. I am obviously not the daughter they wanted. I am an awful person'. Through counselling, she was encouraged to look at her inner relationship with her hurt inner child. She couldn't at first because she hated herself so much! One day it was gently put to her that perhaps she was holding unforgiveness towards her inner child – that she hadn't forgiven her or accepted her with love, for who she was – ie someone very special, loved and accepted by God. At this point tears flowed freely as she came to realise that forgiving her hurt inner child and accepting herself as the person God created her to be was the only way forward. This step enabled her to reconcile the different warring parts of herself. Now she can say for the first time in her life, 'I am enjoying being me'.

Here's another example. One lady recognised in herself a wise self and a little anxious self. When Chris asked whether the wise self could speak to the anxious self the lady said that she couldn't, because she also has a critical self that tells her she can't. The critical voice was destroying a part of her, so she was in constant inner conflict.

It's so interesting because we often simply focus on conflict with other people, at work, home, church etc, but actually there's conflict for many of us within ourselves. We don't like a particular part of ourselves, so we separate it off. It's therefore really important that when we think about conflict we bring in the whole picture, because the conflict that might be going on within ourselves will influence the conflict we have with others. We also need to learn to feed our inner selves with the truths from Scripture, such as: 'there is now no condemnation for those who are in Christ Jesus' (Rom. 8:1) and 'See what great love the Father has lavished on us, that we should be called children of God! And that is what we are!' (1 John 3:1).

ACTIVITY
Try and recognise your own inner voices. What are they saying about you? Are they kind words or destructive words? To what extent do they rule your life? Ask God to help you love and accept yourself just as you are, forgiving your hurt inner child for causing any pain.

HONESTY WITH GOD
We've talked a little about the conflict that we can have with God as well. We saw in the psalm that David had a conflict because he wanted God to do something in a particular way. We too can

be like that. We don't like what God's doing so we demand He does this, that and the other, and end up in conflict with Him. Then we get disappointed and may wonder what the point of praying is.

We will all have our struggles with God over the years and the best thing to do is be honest about it, just like David was. Avoid beating yourself up about the fact that you are having a conflict with God (sometimes we can tell ourselves it's not good, but that causes us to suppress feelings and creates other feelings of unworthiness). It is best to say: 'God, you already know the feelings of my heart so I'm going to be honest with you.' Hear some of the gutsy, honest words of David in another psalm: 'Will the Lord reject for ever? Will he never show his favour again? Has his unfailing love vanished for ever? Has his promise failed for all time? Has God forgotten to be merciful? Has he in his anger withheld his compassion?' (Psa. 77:7–9). Having poured out his pain, David doesn't stop there. He goes on to say, 'I will remember the deeds of the LORD' (v11); 'Your ways, God, are holy. What god is as great as our God?' (v13). Chris has found this psalm very helpful in allowing her to be angry with God when she perceives that God is not answering prayer for a very ill family member. Yet she doesn't stay in that place of anger. Moving on, she praises God for who He is and thanks Him for all His blessings, which she then names. Praying along these lines, Chris has found she doesn't have to pretend to be anyone other than who she is – this is very releasing and comforting.

Claire too has a close family member who has been ill for most of her life. Sometimes it has felt like Claire's own life as a worship leader and pastor's wife, in which she constantly encourages people to reach to God for healing, doesn't match up to the words she is saying. And yet going to God with all her questions and frustrations has allowed her to move forward, and understand that God is still God and still worthy of praise. As a worship leader she has found huge release in taking her difficulties before God and then choosing to sing songs of love and adoration to Him in spite of those things.

As we have both learnt, it is fine to tell God exactly what you think. Recognise that you are human but reiterate that you still love God, and will still trust Him – you just need to be honest with where you are.

REFLECTION
Stop and listen to yourself over the coming week.
- Are you criticising others' failures and faults, without seeing you own?
- When you clash with someone do you stop, listen and try to understand their perception of the situation first?
- Do you excuse yourself by rationalising your behaviour?
- To what extent are your internal voices critical and attacking of self?

Ask the Holy Spirit to shine His light of truth into the crevices of your heart and mind, to reveal any hidden grudges and grievances.

PRAYER
Thank You Lord Jesus that You are the centre of all love and grace. Help me to freely give love and grace to those who hurt me, those I have differences with and those I experience conflict with. Help me to grow in being a channel of Your love. Amen.

CHAPTER FIVE

PRACTICAL SUGGESTIONS FOR CONFLICT SITUATIONS

LEARNING FROM JESUS' EXAMPLE

Before we take a look at how we can actually approach conflict resolution in our own situations it is important to look at what Jesus said and did, because He spoke very directly on this matter.

We believe Jesus taught about this because He was aware of the fallenness of human nature and the hurt we can cause one another. That is why in John 17:20-23 He prays believers may be 'brought to complete unity' so that the world may believe. Disputes and conflict can hinder the work of His kingdom and so Jesus urged His followers to deal with them quickly – and well.

Jesus' teaching in John 13:34 gives us another clue as to how to handle conflict: 'A new command I give you: love one another. As I have loved you, so you must love one another. By this everyone will know that you are my disciples, if you love one another.' God desires love to be the fundamental characteristic of Christians. Larry Crabb said, 'Love is moving towards others without self protection.'[17]

In every situation that could become a conflict it is important to ask ourselves: 'What would Jesus have done?' Why is this important? Well, if Christians can't live alongside one another, being reconciled in love and peace when there is a difference of opinion, how will the world outside our community view us? They probably won't see the love of Jesus in our midst!

If we look at Matthew 18, in verses 15–20 Jesus clearly sets out ways of handling a conflict which we can use when a specific conflict occurs at church – and also transfer the principles to the home and workplace. 'If your brother or sister sins' … He offers three routes to conflict resolution (which follow on after each other), similar in many ways to the three judicial routes that we have today.

The 'out of court' settlement – one to one

Matthew 18:15: 'If your brother or sister sins, go and point out their fault, just between the two of you. If they listen to you, you have won them over.' Sadly, we all know that churches can be places of criticism and backbiting. Indeed, Selwyn Hughes once commented: 'Far too many find fault as if there was a reward in it!'[18]

In this passage Jesus talks about the conflicting parties getting together and working out their differences. Letters, phone calls, emails and texts are less personal and appropriate ways of communication. So, if you are in conflict with someone in the church, start by requesting a face to face with that person.

The source of conflict can often be a lack of understanding and listening. We do not necessarily want the other person to agree – after all he may be right and we may be wrong! But the foundation of any good communication is the ability to listen to one another. Three times the word listen is used here (vv15,16,17).

When trying to resolve conflict, it's about us making that first step to stretch out our hand to try and resolve the issue. As we've said, we are responsible for the way we respond in a conflict situation – how the other party reacts to us reaching out is their responsibility.

Arbitration – seek the help of mediators

Going on to verse 16: 'But if they will not listen, take one or two others along, so that "every matter may be established by the testimony of two or three witnesses."'

This is about requesting the help of impartial witnesses to be mediators and to keep things in perspective (ie by not taking sides). Those who take on this role need to pray, then listen to both sides with humility. When advice is offered, it's essential that both parties come without prejudice, but with the same humility and prayerful attitude.

Confrontation in open court – seek the wisdom of the church

Verse 17 says, 'If they still refuse to listen, tell it to the church'. If nothing has worked to bring about a resolution of the conflict, Jesus says that the person is to be held accountable to the whole church. Obviously, this needs to be done with great sensitivity and doesn't mean making the problem known through the church website or magazine!

In verse 19 it says, 'if two of you on earth agree about anything they ask for, it will be done for them by my Father in heaven'. Our word 'symphony' comes from the Greek *symphonia*, which means 'agreement'. The aim of all of this is for people to come to a harmonious agreement.

If the person with whom you have conflict refuses to listen to the church, then Matthew 18:17 says we should 'treat them as you would a pagan or a tax collector'. We believe this to mean that it's important they are shown love (like Jesus loves the sinner) yet no longer have responsibilities within the Christian community.

Love has to be the bedrock of all conflict resolution. Therefore, learning how to deal with conflict effectively in love is an important life skill; Paul talks about 'speaking the truth in love' (Eph. 4:15). When love is genuine it can withstand disagreements. Conflict without love destroys relationship and damages the church, thus weakening the kingdom of God and our Christian witness.

TACKLE

Because we want to ensure that we deal with our conflicts with an attitude of love and grace, Chris has come up with an acronym that will help you to make a quick and honest self-evaluation, so that you know you are in the right place before you try to resolve what is going on. It also reminds you that you are not alone, so remember to bring God into the equation sooner rather than later!

Trigger: Identify what has triggered or caused the conflict.

Acknowledge the emotions the conflict has stirred up in you, and where they come from (ie are you feeling resentful, bitter, judgmental?).

Consider your own part in the conflict, asking yourself: 'What am I responsible for? What am I going to do with these powerful emotions?' You have a choice – to channel the energy into restoring and building up the relationship or into upsetting the relationship further (spending some time reading through 1 Corinthians 13:4–7 would be helpful at this point too).

Keep asking God for discernment about where the enemy is working in the situation. Satan loves to stir people up against one another and often uses the following approaches: persuading us to focus on trivialities, mannerisms and tone of voice that irritate us or using his lying tongue to accuse us, condemn us and ridicule us.

Lean on God for His help. Ask Him: 'Lord what do You want me to do in this crisis? How can I respond to it in a Christlike manner?' Then make sure you pause and wait for the answer – which can be extremely difficult to do!

Exercise patience: God may well be working both within you and the person with whom you have the rift. Change may be painfully slow, and healing of hurt takes time. Be patient with yourself and the other(s) with whom you are in conflict.

SKILLS USEFUL FOR CONFLICT RESOLUTION
Our ability to resolve conflict will, to some extent, depend upon our communication skills. Learning to be a good listener and cultivating assertiveness skills are extremely useful.

THE USE OF ASSERTIVENESS SKILLS IN CONFLICT
Sometimes, we can be too nice for our own good – and our own health! When we are not assertive we can become people pleasers who play the game 'peace at any price'. We are often driven to say 'yes' to every request and end up looking after other people's needs to the detriment of our own. When we can't say 'no' and are treated as doormats, we can feel resentful towards

those who make demands upon us. Keeping the lid firmly shut on our hidden frustration and anger means that it can then explode at some time and lead to conflict. Our internal world can be a bit like a pressure cooker – the steam of frustration and resentment builds up to such an extent that, with nowhere to go, it blows its top!

Being assertive is not about getting our own way. It is the ability to express one's thoughts, feelings and desires in a way that doesn't abuse others. It is an open, honest and direct communication and, most importantly, assertiveness is a skill that can be learned. Learning to be assertive will help us grow in self-confidence and will enhance our relationships because it gains respect from others. Assertiveness helps maintain the healthy view that we are all of equal worth in God's sight and thus we are all equally deserving of being listened to.

Many people confuse what assertiveness is about and find it difficult to be assertive without first working themselves up into a state of aggressiveness. They think it is about standing one's ground, arguing the point and winning. However, assertiveness is not about winning or losing. Rather it is about finding a compromise so that the end result of any conflict is a win/win situation.

We sometimes end up as non-assertive people because we are frightened of confronting a conflict situation for fear of rejection, or we fear someone else's anger if we say 'no'. We often feel programmed to say 'yes, I'll do that' when we mean the opposite, so learning to buy ourselves some time before we give an answer is vital. If we are being bullied or coerced to do something we don't want to do, then it's important we take a break from the conversation in order to give ourselves 'thinking' time.

Here are some suggestions on how to handle the situation:

- Try to remove yourself physically from face to face contact to break the automatic 'yes' response.
- Go to the bathroom.
- Leave the office.
- Go and get a drink (not alcoholic!).
- Tell the person that you need some time to consider their request before you give them an answer. You might say one of the following:

> 'This doesn't fit comfortably with me at the moment so I need more time to consider it.'
>
> 'Let me come back to you when I've looked at my diary.'
>
> 'I'm not sure if I'll have time to do that: let me see if I can change anything around and I'll come back to you tomorrow.'

- Then, when you return to the person with a 'no', use a 'sandwich' technique. This involves inserting a 'no' between two affirming, complementary or positive statements. You could say:

> 'I appreciate you asking me to do that with you (positive), but on this occasion I won't be able to do it (a 'no'). If I thought I could fit it in, I would (positive). I trust you will understand.'

- Avoid getting into a debate about your decision or thinking you have to justify, explain or excuse your 'no'.

All relationships – good and bad, healthy and unhealthy – involve a measure of conflict. In poor relationships conflict is viewed (and conducted) as a power struggle or control issue with a winner/loser mentality. Hence learning assertiveness skills will help all of us to handle conflict more creatively.[19]

Of course there may be times when you come across someone who just loves to pick a fight for the sake of it (as we have said, some people become addicted to the emotional arousal). In those instances, learning to be assertive can be about refusing to take their bait, and simply walking away from a potential conflict situation.

IMPORTANT COMMUNICATION SKILLS FOR CONFLICT RESOLUTION

During this chapter the word 'listen' has been used several times and has been illustrated by the use of Scripture (Matt. 18). This teaches us how important it is to listen when we are dealing with a conflict, or simply listening to someone who is anxious about a problem. Sometimes we may find that simply listening to the other person's viewpoint helps to diffuse a situation that could have turned into a conflict.

James 1:19 says: 'everyone should be quick to listen, slow to speak and slow to become angry', which suggests that this is a command and not a matter of choice.

Jesus is the perfect example of a good listener: He listened not only with all of His senses but also to His Father (shown by the way that He dealt with the situations that were presented to Him).

Sheila Goldsmith, a 'Christian Listener' of Acorn Christian Healing Foundation (and a close friend of Chris) says, 'We too are called to listen well. Some people are naturally gifted in this way but it is a skill that can be learned and is foundational to all ministries. It's about quality and not quantity, and a service that we can offer to one another.' On one of the Acorn Listening courses that Sheila teaches, she uses a quotation by Dietrich Bonhoeffer: 'The first service one owes to others in fellowship consists in listening to them. Just as the love of God begins with listening to His Word, so the beginning of love for the brothers and sisters is learning to listen to them.'[20]

Listening is the key to all effective communication and is the ability to accurately receive messages in this process. Without effective listening skills, messages are easily misunderstood – communication breaks down and the sender of the message can easily become frustrated and irritated, which may inflame any conflict.

A good listener will listen not only to what is being said, but also to what is not being said. Effective listening involves observing tone of voice, tension in face, body language and noticing inconsistencies between verbal and non-verbal messages.

Reflecting

Part of listening is actively reflecting back what the person has said in order to help them clarify their experience. This is simply echoing their main points using some of their own words. Pick out some of the most pertinent points to show you have been listening. For example: 'You moved to this department four years ago and say since then you have been bullied and hassled' or, 'You dashed back in time to see me and couldn't believe I wasn't here.'

Empathising

Empathising is a very important listening skill because it helps the other person know they are being heard. It is about trying to understand how it feels for the other person, stepping into their shoes and sensing what is going on from their perspective.

(It's not sympathy.) Empathising is about reflecting back feelings, for example: 'From what you've said, I hear that you're feeling overwhelmed and anxious by this situation.' Useful phrases in reflecting feelings include:

It sounds like ... you are disheartened.

I sense that ... perhaps you are feeling anxious because you are not in control.

You seem ... to have mixed feelings about this.

I hear you say that ... you dislike working here.

Summarising

Summarising is a good way of showing that you've heard what a person is saying, and can be useful in punctuating and signposting a discussion, for example: 'You've been telling me about how I treat you badly and how this has an impact on your work. Perhaps we can look at one issue now at a deeper level.'

Clarifying

Sometimes in a conflict situation we are not quite sure what the other person is saying, so we can use phrases to clarify. For example: 'Can we stop for a moment because I'm confused? I'm not sure if you are saying this ... or that ...', 'Can I clarify what I think you're saying?', 'I'm not hearing you say much about the others in the team. Can you tell me more?'

Questioning

Using questioning in conflict resolution is important because it obtains information, provides clarification, it helps those involved to know that they are being listened to and understood, and it can guide thinking.

Good questioning skills are not based on our own judgments or ideas. Here are some guidelines:

- Try not to use questions in an interrogative manner. Avoid asking 'Why?' questions – they are often experienced by others as biased, judgmental and threatening, and will add more fuel to the conflict.
- A constructive way to question is to use one of these words at the beginning of the sentence: 'How?' 'What?' 'When?' or 'Where?' For example: 'How often does this happen?' 'What happened?' 'When did the problem start?' 'Where does this happen?'
- Phrase questions carefully, sensitively and clearly. For example: 'Can you tell me more about what is going on when ...?' 'How do you think this came about?' (Rather than 'Why do you think this came about?') 'Would you like to tell me more about where you think we differ about this issue?'
- Questions can be a way of checking things out, 'I'm not sure I have quite understood you. Can you tell me more?'

The basis of any good communication is the ability to employ all these helpful skills, because they will help towards resolving the conflict.

PRACTICAL STRATEGIES FOR CONFLICT RESOLUTION SITUATIONS

Now we are going to look at some suggestions for how to try to resolve conflict with another person, including how to approach them and what to avoid.

Creating a healthy atmosphere for conflict resolution

Creating an effective atmosphere in which conflict can be resolved is an important skill. Atmosphere is like the weather around us; it can affect how we feel and act. Thus an environment where we feel safe, in order to look at our differences and work out how to improve the relationship, is of the utmost importance. We know that God wants us to interact with others with love, so how do we create an atmosphere of love when we are in conflict with them? Here are some suggestions that will impact the atmosphere as you talk things through with the other party.

Timing
Choose a mutually convenient time, rather than demanding a time that isn't agreeable to the other person, otherwise you may set up some conflict before you even start! Be wise and choose a time that maximises concentration and communication, so don't suggest meeting late at the end of a really busy day. Also be aware of how long the talking goes on without a break. Is the talking just going round and round in circles? It's important to set a deadline for the meeting to end, because this is more likely to influence an outcome. You may want to suggest going away and coming back another time if it goes on too long.

Location
Think about what may be a safe location for you (ie not in the office in front of all your other colleagues). While some couples choose to talk things through in a café or other public place as it ensures their voices do not escalate to anger, it is often better to choose a quieter spot. Look for a place that is peaceful and non-threatening to all parties. It needs to be somewhere quiet and devoid of distractions or diversions and somewhere that will not offend any cultural differences.

For example, it could be that you meet in an appropriate room within your workplace, such as a designated dialogue room, rather than in the manager's office. Try to create a circular seating place, as tables can be symbols of rigid division. The following example highlights this. Chris was working with a young teenage girl who was in a lot of conflict at school because of what was going on in the rest of her life (so some of it was very understandable). But when the girl and her mother were invited to meet with the head teacher to talk the issues through, they found the seating logistics added to their discomfort. The head was seated on one side of a great big square table, and they had to sit opposite her on the other side. Mother and daughter felt they were being treated as the naughty ones – they described it as 'so confrontational' – and that was just the seating arrangements! They felt it would have been more conducive to talking if they had been seated in a circle without a table in the middle. Locations may not create the necessary atmosphere for talking and rather than resolving conflict, can sometimes make it worse.

Opening words
When beginning any conversation with the intent of resolving conflict, it is very important not to start with negative or confrontational phrases. It is much better to start with something positive, such as 'I value our relationship so I want to clear the air'. Then move on to establish a relationship of 'we'. In many instances you may want to remind people that 'we are in this together' and that 'we want to work, side by side, to find a resolution'. Dispelling the fear that we are viewing the process as an 'I' versus 'you' battle or 'I want to destroy you to make a conquest' will smooth the path to resolution. Something like this could be said:

'I want you to know that I am not seeing this conflict as a struggle for who becomes a winner or who is to blame. We are in this together, and I want both of us to feel some of our needs are being met and that our relationship will grow because of this time together.'

Affirm the other person for who they are:

'I really appreciate that you are trustworthy, kind and have a lot of wisdom.' (Make sure this is true and don't patronise!)

Affirm the belief that options, alternative ways and realistic steps for improvement can be created through a shared effort. So let them know that you are open to exploring the issues and their suggestions and you want to work on these together:

'We probably have both thought of how we can approach things differently, and I am sure that together we can creatively explore new options and ways of doing things.'

Show an interest in the relationship overall, while acknowledging that there is a conflict:

'I value our relationship and acknowledge that this conflict just affects one aspect. I am sure we can work together to improve things and learn how to handle any other problems we may face in the future as well.'

Let the other person know that it is OK to be able to agree and disagree on a particular matter:

'I really want to learn from you in this disagreement and hopefully there will be things you can learn from me. Just because we disagree about something, doesn't mean we have to negate the good things we share together in our relationship.'

It also may be relevant to say:

'I know I lost my temper for which I apologise. It seemed that we both became angry and made some impossible demands. I am encouraged that we are able to work together to try and find a more constructive way to resolve this issue.'

Continuing dialogue

When trying to resolve a conflict it is important to distinguish between fact and opinion. So when you first start talking, try to stick to the facts only. 'I hear that you are upset about me not getting that piece of work done on time.' Then when you move on, start talking about personal opinions, rather than stating those things as facts. Use phrases such as: 'I am aware I think differently to you', 'As I understand it', 'As I experience it', 'I do not agree with that summary' or 'I am conscious that'. Try not to be judgmental, accuse or condemn. Use these phrases: 'I've noticed recently that' or 'I find that unacceptable'. Only after covering those things should you talk about how you are feeling: 'I'm feeling disappointed about this', 'I'm confused about this', 'I feel sad that we can't see eye to eye'. All these phrases are useful tools in handling conflict because they don't apportion blame.

Learning when to end

While it is important to keep talking and exploring the issue, there will also come a time when it's important to stop. This may be because you have reached a mutually agreeable resolution, which is great, but there could be other reasons. As already mentioned, if you are not getting anywhere or if it is getting late, call it a day and arrange another mutually convenient time. This could also give you both time to mull over what has been said or not said and think about the way forward.

On other hand, the other person could become very aggressive (which we will be covering later on in this chapter). You may find that they are simply not entering into the supposed conflict resolution with the right spirit; you may feel that they are becoming too personal and emotions are beginning to hit a 'hot spot'.

Chris has found that she has had to teach people to say: 'I am not prepared to stay and listen to this personal attack on me. I am worth more than standing here listening to your words, so I'm going to leave the room.' If someone is throwing a lot of unhelpful muck at you it's important to hold on to who you are and say to yourself, 'I don't have to stand here and soak this up like a sponge, I can remove myself.' For those of us who are people pleasers it can be particularly important to learn to say to the other person, 'I'm worth more than listening to your constant criticism, and I'm not taking that on board' then remove ourselves from their presence so they can't fire any more bullets at us.

The other reason you may need to stop is because you realise you are never going to see eye to eye. In these situations it is okay to say: 'I respect your value system and want to respect you as another human. We seem to have come to a bit of an impasse here so I am not sure about continuing this conversation.' It may mean changing something drastically or choosing to discontinue working towards a resolution. Whatever decision you come to, it's really important to have non-judgmental acceptance when you feel you have reached a cul-de-sac.

Summary of guidelines
- Start by affirming that you are working together to improve your relationship and work out the differences – then the interaction becomes a partnership.
- When referring to the conflict, first talk about the facts, then opinions, expectations and differences, then how you feel about this.
- Don't use 'you' statements (such as, 'you make me very mad'). Using 'you' immediately makes the other person go into defensive mode – they are more likely to throw muck back at you and then the conflict escalates. Use 'I' statements, such as 'I am feeling sad/angry/about this situation.'
- Be specific, stating your complaint as objectively as possible.
- Focus on the person's behaviour that is causing the tension, rather than criticising them as a person.
- Don't over-generalise, eg 'You're always doing this ...'
- Talk about one issue at a time.
- Be open to criticism.
- Be open and accepting of differences.
- Relationship building and conflict resolution are interconnected.
- Remind yourself that conflict doesn't have to be negative.
- Take responsibility for your anger and your part in the conflict.
- Be aware of putting yourself down ('I know that I nag') and avoid it.

- Don't invite retaliatory anger: 'I know you will shout at me when I tell you.'
- Bringing up past grievances is a 'no, no' as it will cause even more anger.
- Don't label, mind read, preach or moralise.
- Be careful not to make idle threats.
- Don't see the resolution as win or lose. Try find a way that both parties can have their needs met.
- Think the issues through carefully.
- Don't predict what the outcome must be.
- Pray – surrender the outcome to God.

ACTIVITY

Think of a conflict situation. If you don't want to use one of your own personal conflicts, you could try the following scenario: two team members are disagreeing about how to run the church kids' club; both have very fixed ideas on what they think is best.

Take some time to brainstorm some of the ways in which they could resolve their conflict. Concentrate on what approach you think could be best, and what sort of terminology/phraseology would be appropriate. Below are some ideas and questions to help you as necessary.

- **Clarify perceptions**

  What is this conflict about? Clarify the contentious issues rather than focusing on the emotions involved.

  Get each person to think: Is it about me? The other person? Or both of us?

  What are the relational styles – avoider, winner, aggressor etc?

  What are our priorities in sorting this conflict out?

- **Develop a common vision** (this appeals to people's feelings and will).

  Get them to work together – even with the whole team – to focus on developing a vision. They could ask themselves the following questions as individuals as well as a group:

  What catchphrase, slogan, or purpose statement would this team like to adopt to illustrate to others something about its function? What three principles would the team choose to help them work together?

  If something was suggested that was contrary to my values, would I stand firm and not compromise?

  What changes would I have to make to bring this vision to reality?

- **Discuss the less emotive questions first**

  Getting too caught up in the emotions to begin with will make the whole process much harder, so leave emotive issues until later.

- **Break down the issue into components**

  It can be a lot easier to handle conflicts if they are broken down into smaller elements that are much more straightforward to deal with. Working on small achievable goals will be easier than trying to work on the whole issue in one go.

HOW TO HANDLE ESCALATING ANGER

One of the most difficult things about any dialogue involving conflict is that either or both of the parties can become angry very quickly. We are going to take a look at how to handle your own anger – and what to do if the other person becomes angry.

Some of it has already been touched upon, but this can be such a huge thing within dialogue over conflict that it is important to cover it more fully here.

How to handle your own anger

If you recognise that a conflict situation is starting to brew, and you can sense you are beginning to get angry, then there are things you can do to help yourself calm down.

Stop when you notice minor irritation within yourself. (You may become increasingly irritated by what the other person is saying or doing.)

Check your body for signs of tension. It might be that your stomach starts to feel strange, or you have palpitations in your chest. Those sorts of things indicate that you are beginning to get uptight and the adrenalin is pumping around your body.

Release your physical tension by doing the breathing exercise described in chapter 2. Depending upon where you are, you may have to do it standing up.

Analyse what is going on. Here are some questions you could ask yourself in order to do this:

1. Does this situation remind me of any other? Has an old wound been opened?

2. Do I feel threatened? If so, am I perceiving this rationally or am I exaggerating it?

3. Are so many demands being made of me that I am feeling stressed?

4. Am I taking responsibility for my own behaviour? Is my perspective coloured or distorted? Am I personalising what is being said?

Don't put off expressing how you feel for long periods and

withdraw into silence – ruminating on thoughts and feelings in the silence will increase emotional arousal.

Prepare your words carefully to open up a discussion that will hopefully lead to some resolution, or, at the very least, inform the other person of your feelings. Think about what to say, and what not to say, so that you are prepared.

David was a young professional who had been happily married for three years. However, he was becoming increasingly hostile towards his wife. One day, without any provocation, he lashed out. He was very distressed and confused about his behaviour; after all, he loved his wife. She had done nothing to deserve this.

He began to explore what was going on inside his inner world and at first, could find no connection with any possible trigger. His counsellor encouraged him to think back to when he first felt any tension in his body, or any bodily discomfort, and note when this first started. After some consideration, he remembered. He had a racing heart and mounting pressure in his head once he had boarded a train on his return journey from visiting his father.

His parents had been very happily married for the first five years of David's life and then suddenly their relationship went sour. This unhappy environment dragged on into his teens until eventually his parents went through a very acrimonious divorce. He had always felt that somehow he was to blame for his parents' split. Guilt kicked in and he became angry with himself. His visit to see his father triggered these underlying feelings. Hitting his wife was his way of releasing these negative and destructive emotions.

After the source was uncovered, David was able to work through these feelings, which was the key for resolving his inner conflict and restoring his relationship with his wife.

How to handle explosive anger in yourself

- Withdraw from the situation and calm down. Sometimes we feel we are going to literally explode with anger. Nothing that is said in such a state is helpful (and you may also lash out physically by throwing something or even trying to hit the person). So it would be best for you to remove yourself from the situation by simply saying: 'I'm getting so worked up at the moment that I can't think straight, so I'm going to go out and withdraw myself for around twenty minutes and then I'll come back and perhaps we can pick it up then.' Did you know that it can take anything from fifteen to thirty minutes for our emotions and racing adrenalin to calm down?

- During time out, don't spend time rehearsing the grievances because that will keep the physiological arousal going. Instead, do something that is distracting and relaxing. Don't get on the phone to your best friend and go over and over how awful the other person is! This will only maintain the anger. Adrenalin, as we have mentioned, is pumping round our body when we get worked up and it's important that we have a strategy to manage this, and thus calm our body down. So try doing something calming like take a walk, have a hot drink, engage the part of your mind not focused on the situation with something else and/or try some calming breathing exercises see chapter 2 or relaxation.

How to handle explosive anger in others

When the person with whom you are trying to resolve a conflict is beginning to explode you need to postpone your conversation. Here are some pointers on what to do to keep the situation from escalating and how to get out of it safely. Some of this is based on what Chris learnt from talking to a policeman in her church. We will first identify the warning and danger signs of conflict, then look at how to manage this.

Warning signs of a potential threat:

- Direct prolonged eye contact
- Increased breathing rate
- Exaggerated limb movements
- Head back
- Kicking something – transfer of aggression

Danger signs:

- Clenched fists
- Hand risen above the waist
- Teeth clenched and lips tightened
- Shoulders tense
- Stance changed from front on to side on – fighting stance
- Facial colour pales

Having identified a potential threat, consider the way forward:

- What options are open to me (available resources and support, own knowledge and experience)?
- How probable is the risk of harm?
- How serious would that be?
- Is that level of risk acceptable?
- Am I the appropriate person to deal with this?

- Is this a situation for the police to deal with?
- What am I trying to achieve?

The way to respond:

- *Keep cool*

The worst thing you can do is match the other person's escalating anger with noise yourself. Try to keep calm.

- *Speak slowly with eye contact*

It is important to speak very slowly and give a little eye contact in order to indicate that you are listening (but not looking at them constantly or they will think they've got your full attention and could become even more aggressive, pouring out their increasing anger upon you). If you speak quickly by matching their speed and tone, this can also increase their aggression. So it's important to deliberately lower your speed and pitch of voice.

- *Positive self talk*

Say something positive to yourself, such as: 'I have some skills to handle this difficult situation' or 'It probably won't turn out as bad as I'm thinking'.

- *Share your own feelings and fears*

Let them know that their behaviour is causing you to be anxious and you are fearful that they may do something that you will both regret. Say something like: 'I am frightened because I feel you are losing control.'

- *Check your physical position*

This is extremely important advice from the police: if you feel the conflict is getting out of hand then make sure there is something between you and the other person as a means of protection.

- *Keep your eyes open for something to throw*

If you feel you need to get out quickly then throw something away from your means of exit in order to divert the other person's attention long enough to allow you to get out. Use something that will make a noise – this will make it easier to distract them, and may also alert other people to what is going on. If you are feeling trapped and are not near the door, consider using a window instead, as long as you can do so safely.

- *If things get out of control – ie physical aggression*

Activate 999 on your mobile or landline, as an open line can assist the police in understanding what's going on. If you can covertly ring 999, and the other person is unaware, then you can say something like, 'Stop hitting me' and the call taker may be able to hear this and trace the number (not guaranteed).

ACTIVITY

The following is a list of some of the main conflict strategies that we have looked at in this book. Hopefully you will feel that you are equipped to do these things now, but do take your time and read through them slowly and honestly. If there are any that you don't yet feel confident about, go back and work through the relevant part of the book.

- Recognise the signs of conflict in self, others and the environment (chapter 1).
- Recognise when you are trying to meet your spiritual needs in other ways, other than in God, and how this causes blocked goals (chapter 2).
- Recognise how thoughts, beliefs and perceptions, as well as value systems and beliefs, can add fuel to conflicts (see chapter 3).
- Learn to approach conflict with grace, forgiveness and peace as the ultimate goal (chapter 4).

- Learn to love and accept yourself, thus being gracious and forgiving of yourself (chapter 4).
- Know when it is time to let go of trying to reconcile with someone who doesn't want it (chapter 4).
- Learn to ask the question 'Where is God in this conflict?' (chapters 2 and 4).
- Remind yourself how to approach conflict using TACKLE (chapter 5).
- Be able to use good communication skills when engaged in conflict resolution (chapter 5).
- Learn the importance of creating the right atmosphere for conflict resolution (chapter 5).
- Learn practical skills to handle your own and others' anger (chapter 5).
- Be honest and ask yourself the question: Do I have a conflict or does the conflict have me?

KEEPING GOD AT THE CENTRE

Conflict can be seen as a gift from God; it can initiate positive change but shouldn't control our reaction to it. It's about learning strategies to help us resolve conflict whenever we can. It's about creatively moving forward in difficult decisions.

Always remember that as a Christian you have a great ally in God. You are not doing this by yourself, so you can draw on God's wisdom and strength, and remember that we love because He first loved us. Make it a personal goal to continually reflect on the fact that God loves you and accepts you as you are. And then: 'If it is possible, as far as it depends on you, live at peace with everyone' (Rom. 12:18).

REFLECTION

Read and meditate on the extract below, from 1 Corinthians 13:4–7, *The Message*.

> Love never gives up.
>
> Love cares more for others than for self.
>
> Love doesn't want what it doesn't have.
>
> Love doesn't strut,
>
> Doesn't have a swelled head,
>
> Doesn't force itself on others,
>
> Isn't always 'me first',
>
> Doesn't fly off the handle,
>
> Doesn't keep score of the sins of others,
>
> Doesn't revel when others grovel,
>
> Takes pleasure in the flowering of truth,
>
> Puts up with anything,
>
> Trusts God always,
>
> Always looks for the best,
>
> Never looks back,
>
> But keeps going to the end.

Think back over the conflict situations you have been involved in, and reflect on how your attitudes and actions compared to the above. Were you able to take the love of God with you into the conflict? If not, what were you trying to achieve?

PRAYER

Let's finish this book by turning our hearts towards God, regardless of any conflict situation we are facing, and praise and thank Him for His goodness and love:

Father, thank You that we are all so different – we're like the different instruments playing a symphony. Just as those instruments create a beautiful sound, You want us to live in harmony with one another. Help me to grow in the areas of reflecting Your love and handling conflict well. May my roots grow deep into the soil of Your love, so that in any conflict situation I glorify Your name. Amen.

APPENDIX 1

Different responses to conflict

Tick the responses that best describe your reaction to disagreement and disputes.

- ☐ Withdraw/become silent
- ☐ Criticise or use sarcasm
- ☐ Negotiate/compromise
- ☐ Give in
- ☐ Force your own way upon others
- ☐ Hide your real feelings
- ☐ Evade the issue
- ☐ Stop when beginning to lose the argument
- ☐ Agree to differ
- ☐ Pretend the problem doesn't exist
- ☐ Share your thoughts and feelings
- ☐ Blame: 'You always … You never …'
- ☐ Procrastinate/too busy to talk
- ☐ Explore the issue openly
- ☐ Become resentful
- ☐ Often use the 'I' statements
- ☐ Often use the 'you' statements
- ☐ Threaten the other person (physically, emotionally, verbally)
- ☐ Exaggerate the problem
- ☐ Work towards a just resolution of the conflict

APPENDIX 2

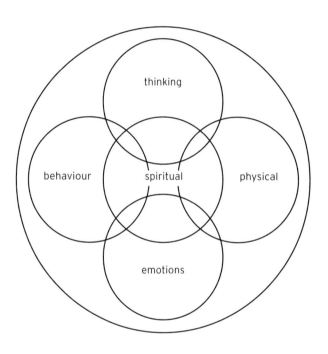

APPENDIX 3

Murder

Suicide

Abuse

Hatred   Threaten

Bitterness   Intimidate

Resentment   Insult

Unforgiveness   Slander   **ACTIVE**
                             FORMS OF
Repugnance   Incite   **ANGER**

Contempt   Humiliate

PASSIVE   Disgust   Sneer
FORMS OF
ANGER   Jealousy   Criticise

Envy   Sarcasm

Frustration   Spite

Annoyance

Moodiness

Sullen Silence

APPENDIX 4

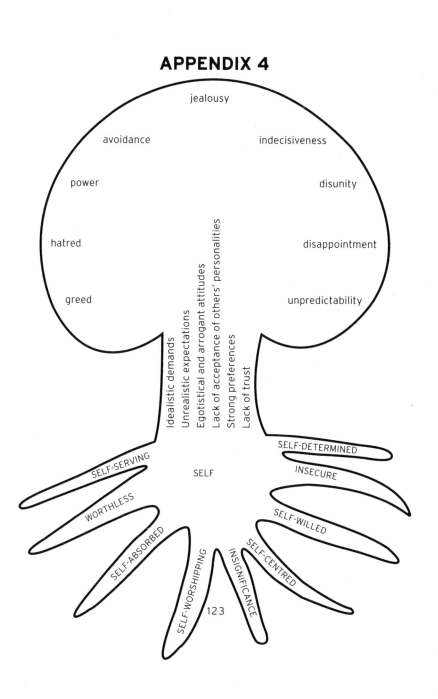

jealousy

avoidance

indecisiveness

power

disunity

hatred

disappointment

greed

unpredictability

Idealistic demands
Unrealistic expectations
Egotistical and arrogant attitudes
Lack of acceptance of others' personalities
Strong preferences
Lack of trust

SELF-DETERMINED

SELF-SERVING

INSECURE

SELF

WORTHLESS

SELF-WILLED

SELF-ABSORBED

SELF-CENTRED

SELF-WORSHIPPING

INSIGNIFICANCE

123

NOTES

1   *Collins English Dictionary & Thesaurus* (Glasgow: HarperCollins
    Publishers, 2006) and *Compact Oxford English Dictionary*,
    (Oxford: Oxford University Press, 1996).

2   Ruth Gledhill, 'Petty squabbles cause empty pews', *The Times*,
    25 August 2005.

3   To go into this subject in more detail, do read one of Berne's own
    books, such as Eric Berne, *Games People Play* (London: Penguin
    Books, 2010 – originally published 1964).

4   Taken from tccr.ac.uk/policy/policy-briefings/267-impact-of-couple-
    conflict-on-children-tccr-policy-briefing
    The two sources cited within this are: Harold, G. T., Pryor, J., and
    Reynolds, J. *Not in front of the children? How conflict between parents
    affects children* (One-Plus-One Marriage and Partnership Research:
    London, 2001) and Harold, G. T., Aitken, J. J. and Shelton, K. H., 'Inter-
    parental conflict and children's academic attainment: a longitudinal
    analysis', *Journal of Child Psychology and Psychiatry*, 48, 2007.

5   In 2012 Professor Nathan Fox of the University of Maryland undertook
    research in Romania. His findings include some heartbreaking facts:
    'Effects of institutionalization can be long-lasting and children who
    have been moved to family care still face lower IQs, deficits in language
    use and executive function, exhibit impairments and social-emotional
    problems and a high prevalence of mental health problems.' Quote taken
    from: http://www.newsdesk.umd.edu/big/release.cfm?ArticleID=2743

6   You can read more about this in Chris's book (co-authored with
    Christine Orme), *Insight into Assertiveness* (Surrey: CWR, 2009).
    See the section on 'Selfish versus selfless', p40.

7   Joyce Huggett, *Conflict* (Guildford: Eagle, Inter Publishing Service
    (IPS) Ltd, 1998) p129.

8   Aristotle quote taken from http://www.brainyquote.com/quotes/
    authors/a/aristotle.html

9   William Secker, from *The Nonsuch Professor in His Meridian Splendor*,
    or the Singular Actions of Sanctified Christians (1660) – found on
    www.allthingswilliam.com.

10 Matthew Ostow's quote from Tim LaHaye, *Anger is a Choice*
    (Grand Rapids, MI; Zondervan Publishing House, 1982), p51 where it